JUL 1 0 2023

SIXTY-ONE

SIXTY-CHRIS

ONE PAUL

LIFE LESSONS FROM PAPA,
ON AND OFF THE COURT

WITH MICHAEL WILBON

ST. MARTIN'S PRESS
NEW YORK

First published in the United States by St. Martin's Press,
an imprint of St. Martin's Publishing Group

SIXTY-ONE. Copyright © 2023 by Christopher Emmanuel
Paul and Michael Wilbon. All rights reserved. Printed in
the United States of America. For information, address
St. Martin's Publishing Group,
120 Broadway, New York, NY 10271.

www.stmartins.com

Designed by Devan Norman

Library of Congress Cataloging-in-Publication Data

Names: Paul, Chris, 1985– author. | Wilbon, Michael, author.
Title: Sixty-one : life lessons from papa, on and off the
    court / Chris Paul, with Michael Wilbon.
Description: First edition. | New York : St. Martin's Press,
    2023.
Identifiers: LCCN 2022021228 | ISBN 9781250276711
    (hardcover) | ISBN 9781250276728 (ebook) |
    ISBN 9781250290854 (signed edition)
Subjects: LCSH: Paul, Chris, 1985– | Paul, Chris, 1985––
    Family. | Grandparent and child. | Community life—North
    Carolina—Winston-Salem. | Winston-Salem (N.C.)—
    Biography.
Classification: LCC GV884.P376 A3 2023 | DDC 796.323092
    [B]—dc23/eng/20220604
LC record available at https://lccn.loc.gov/2022021228

Our books may be purchased in bulk for promotional,
educational, or business use. Please contact your local
bookseller or the Macmillan Corporate and Premium Sales
Department at 1-800-221-7945, extension 5442, or by email
at MacmillanSpecialMarkets@macmillan.com.

First Edition: 2023

10 9 8 7 6 5 4 3 2 1

To Papa Chilly

CONTENTS

CONTENTS

CONTENTS

A grandfather is someone with silver in
his hair and gold in his heart.

—Author Unknown

SIXTY-ONE

1

THE GAME

-- -- -- -- -- -- -- -- -- -- -- -- -- -- -- -- --

Parkland High School, Winston-Salem
Parkland vs. West Forsyth High
November 20, 2002

It was the first game of my senior season, and I wasn't even sure if I was going to play. Imagine that, the game I loved more than anything, my happy place, and I didn't want to touch a basketball.

We were about to play against Parkland High

School, where my mom and her sister, my aunt Rhonda, had gone. They were the only two people in our family that went to Parkland. Everybody else went to Carver High School, a "Black" school over in East Winston, which had a reputation for being a lot tougher than other schools. My older brother, CJ, and I were big-time athletes at West Forsyth, a high school on the other side of town, which was pretty much a "white" school.

My grandfather, Papa Chilly, as we called him, wasn't going to be there. I always looked forward to seeing his smile and his energy when I looked up in the crowd. I had no idea how I was going to go out on the court, knowing that I wouldn't be able to glance in the stands and see him cheering me on.

Somehow, some way, I built up the energy to attend school that day. Attendance was a requirement for playing, so at least I checked that box, but I didn't hang around in the gym afterward like I usually did. Instead, I went straight to the house.

I knew my aunt Rhonda would be there, and either Mom or Dad, or both, depending on who wasn't working, along with a bunch of my family members visiting from D.C. and Virginia. When I got home, everybody was there hanging out on the upstairs deck eating, reminiscing, chillin', and catching up.

"Hey, Chris, how you feeling?" Aunt Rhonda asked. "What time is the game later?"

"We play at Parkland at seven. We'll see," I answered. They didn't know I was struggling with whether or not to play, but once I saw my family, I knew I had to play. I kept trading hugs and fist bumps with aunts and uncles. They gave me the regular "Boy, you are getting big!" or "Robin, what are you feeding these kids?!" type of commentary that you get when you find yourself in front of family you haven't seen in a minute.

"I'm glad you're playing," Aunt Rhonda said. "He would have wanted you to."

"Okay, Auntie," I responded.

"Papa loves seeing you play," Aunt Rhonda said, with tears streaming down her face. "Why don't you do something special for your granddad?"

I started to think about a couple of ways I could honor my grandfather. Papa always had taken great care of CJ and me—really our whole family, but I had no idea specifically about what I should be doing for him in that moment. Some guys dedicated games, even whole seasons to loved ones. Others wrote important family members' names or meaningful symbols on the sides of their sneakers, hid them in the seams of their jerseys, or even got tattoos. It seemed easy for most people to figure out ways to honor the ones they cared about, so why was I struggling? What was mine?

2

PAPA

— — — — — — — — — — — — — — — — — — — —

I'M BLESSED AND HIGHLY FAVORED.

—PAPA CHILLY

Now listen, I can guarantee you one thing: my Papa had the dirtiest hands you'd ever seen in your life.

The tips of his fingernails all the way down to the ends of his palms were stained with never-ending grease. The discoloration was earned from the years of burying his hands in the grease, oil, and filth that make up a life lived in an auto shop. Most mechanics would wear gloves, but not my granddad. With his bare hands, he would lift whole engines by himself like a gladiator and place them into the cars he fixed, cars that other garages might have written off. My real-life superhero. Papa didn't write off any cars—he could fix anything that was towed, tugged, or pushed into the shop. Those same stained hands were legendary and had as much if not more of an impact on our family and community than anything I can do on a basketball court. Those dirty hands seemed to bother CJ and me a lot more than they bothered Papa. Day in and day out, he'd soak them in a gallon-size bucket of paste-textured yellow soap and scrub them religiously, all the while knowing good and well that that soap wasn't doing a damn thing.

You remember that scene from *The Original Kings of Comedy*? The one where Cedric the Entertainer is doing the impression of the old guy from the neighborhood who's always talking with a cigarette hanging out the corner of his mouth? Well, that's my Papa, that is him through and through.

Even if you're too young to remember or don't know that reference, if you're from the South, you definitely know this guy. Every neighborhood had this guy. You could find him out on the block, at your local auto repair shop, or maybe in front of the Pep Boys. You pull up in a car that has a janky engine, and he comes strolling out, wiping his hands with that greasy red rag.

"Can you fix it, sir?" you nervously ask, noticing those filthy engine-fixing hands, thinking how this guy must spend his time resurrecting cars all day. "Can you?"

"Can I *fix* it? Boy, I been here thirty years. Been here longer than you been alive. Of course I can fix it. Come on, now. I know a carburetor problem when I see it. Bring it 'round here."

Except it doesn't sound like that at all, because somehow he's speaking in complete sentences while smoking a Winston cigarette at the same time. It sounds something like, "Canahfixit? Beenherethirtyoddyearnow. Courseicanfixit. Cmonnah knowadang carburetorproblemwhen ahseeitnow. Brangitinna*grage*."

Cigarette flipping every which way as he's talking, breaking the laws of physics, smoke flying all around his head, ashes falling onto the ground.

That was my grandfather. That was Papa to a tee, and I loved every bit of it.

My grandfather Nathaniel Frederick Jones, Papa, or Chilly, as he was called, was always unapologetically himself, and we loved him for that. Why Chilly? Well, he was the sixth and exact middle child of eleven and his mom always used to call him "Sugar." One of his brothers, Odell, couldn't pronounce "Sugar" so he called Papa "Shilly." Later when he married my grandma Rachel, she had a hard time pronouncing "Shilly" so it turned into "Chilly" and that one stuck.

Papa was born and raised in Winston-Salem, North Carolina, and was always proud to let you know. At six feet two inches, he wasn't a giant; however, he had a spirit fit for a man that stands taller than ten feet. It showed every time he would walk into a room, giving contagious energy with his magnetic smile, his funny stories—he just had such presence. Everyone knew or wanted to know Papa, and so many people relied on him.

I recall countless occasions where family, friends, or community members rolled up on him like, "Mr. Jones, I need some help," and it didn't matter if it involved money for an electric bill, to buy some clothes, to get some food, or whatever they needed to get by—Papa was there. He'd dig those generous hands deep into his pockets, pull out a wad of cash, gladly peeling the person's problem away, bill by bill. Papa didn't ask to be paid back or ask you to listen to a lecture before helping, and he wanted nothing in return. He thought it was a blessing to be a blessing.

No matter what was going on, whenever anyone asked, "Hey, Jones, how you doing?" or "What's up, Chilly? How you feelin' today?" one thing came out of his mouth: "I'm blessed and highly favored." That's how he went about his life; he truly believed that and felt that every day. Maybe it started in Southern churches because a lot of Black people say *I'm blessed and highly favored* all the time—meaning that because you're here living, you've been chosen by God, and if that's the case, then how bad can things really be?

Papa proudly owned Jones Chevron. As far as we knew, his station was the first Black-owned service station in North Carolina. Most people who knew my grandfather always connected him with this, but they didn't know that Jones Chevron was actually his second service station.

Papa's original business was called Jones Gulf, and it was located off Claremont Avenue on the northeast side of Winston-Salem. Early on, Papa was just proud to establish himself as a business owner at Jones Gulf, but as he got more into the business and learned how things worked, he became frustrated. By not owning the land his station sat on, he didn't truly own his business. This was a big problem, and he knew it. For years, Papa tried to buy the land from its white property owner, but that guy was hell-bent on not selling that land to a Black person. Sure, it was okay with the landlord if a Black man rented the property and paid him for that privilege, but there was no way he wanted to give him a chance to actually own the land. Unfortunately, these things still happen today. The great thing about my papa is that no one, not even that landlord, could deny him a chance to do anything. Papa was a worker, a real hard worker who didn't believe in handouts. He knew that by working hard he could make his dreams come true, and that's what he did. He patiently waited for a service station to become available, closed the doors to Jones Gulf, and signed the mortgage on Jones Chevron. His *own* mortgage. And he was damn proud of it.

My mom and Aunt Rhonda didn't know Papa was buying the service station. Papa's wife, my grandma, Rachel H. Jones, picked them up from school like usual. On a normal day, she'd swing past the ice cream shop to treat them and then take them to see Papa at the station. That day, however, Grandma Rachel got the girls the ice cream, but as they were getting close to the station, Grandma made a different turn.

"Wait, why aren't we headed to see Daddy?" my mom asked. "The shop is the other way, right?"

"We're not going to the Gulf, baby. And we won't be going there no more," Grandma replied with a smile, locking eyes with my mother through the rearview mirror. The three of them pulled up to a new station, where Papa was out front, standing tall and brushing off the shoulder of his blue work suit. He was staring at a huge, bright white sign that read JONES CHEVRON.

The excited new employees, dressed like Papa and happy to be working for him at the new station, were gazing at the sign as well, a satisfied look of accomplishment across all their faces.

"Daddy! Daddy! What's that?" my mother screamed as she jumped out of Grandma's sedan, Aunt Rhonda right behind her.

Papa bear-hugged his two young princesses before pulling back to look at them.

"This is for our family business; we own the station, and now we own the land too. This is what I worked for," Papa said. "This belongs to us."

My mother broke away and ran her fingers across the huge Jones Chevron sign, poking at the logo, noticing the texture of the smooth, cold plastic. She looked up at him, beaming with pride.

"It's ours," Papa said to both of his girls, before looking at the other two guys in the blue work suits. "Let's get to work!"

To this day, I can still remember the phone number at the station. It was 723-2232. And every time you answered the phone, you had to say, "Jones Chevron."

Back then, people thought about gas stations like a rest stop, or a place to get candy, coffee, soda, cigarettes, lottery tickets, or beer, but Papa's was different.

Being there felt and smelled like home—it was a family business in every sense of the word. Papa employed the best mechanics in the area, all trained by him, and they loved making customers feel comfortable and appreciated. It was a master class in service in a way I never seen from a mechanic or service station before or since. Imagine your transmission slipping and not even being bothered a little, because you knew Mr. Jones and his crew were going to take care of you. They weren't going to take advantage of you or charge you for things that you didn't need. "Make sure you check your fluids and keep the oil changed," Papa would tell clients, whom he treated like extended family. "That's the best way to protect that engine."

All of Papa's employees rotated tires, changed oil, performed tune-ups, fixed alternators, installed brakes and rotors, and even went as far as swapping whole engines in and out. Everything and anything around cars, they did so well. Jones Chevron also performed state inspections, which back then used to cost $19.40. I'll always remember that price—you know why? Because most people would pay with a twenty-dollar bill and tell CJ and me to keep the sixty cents' change. Every little bit helped when you were saving to buy a grape soda or a Dr. Pepper to go with your Honeybun from the vending machine around back. If it was a good day, you might even have a quarter left over to buy a gumball too. Back in those days, the money added up quickly because a lot of people came to us for inspections.

At most places, you would never, ever pass inspection if you had windows tinted too dark, but that didn't bother us, not one bit. We always took care of people with dark tints, so they always came back to us. Because they thought dark tints should be legal, people just threw them on anyway after they passed inspections, and CJ and I needed some way to keep that sixty-cent soda train running.

One of my parents would drop us off at the station, which was about twenty minutes away from our home on the other side of town. Sometimes they would take us to the station as early as 6:00 a.m. We would get all into it like we really worked there, and in our minds we really did—we'd even go so far as to drink coffee with Papa every single morning. Papa's coffee contained enough sugar to put you into a diabetic coma. There was so much sugar that if you put a spoon in there, it'd stand straight up. It was so sweet that I could feel a cavity as soon as I was done drinking it, but that didn't matter, I was doing what Papa did. To this day, I still can't drink coffee and I have no doubt that it's because I overdosed at the station.

Starting when I was six and CJ was eight, all the way until high school, if we weren't playing football and basketball, or at church, we were probably at the station. While hanging around the shop, CJ and I gained so many life lessons from Papa and his crew; the opportunity to watch Papa in action paid the most dividends.

When I say, "My granddad owned a service station that doubled as an auto repair shop," people think of him as an owner, right? You'd think that he would be sitting back in a recliner, chillin' and watching everyone else do the work, but that wasn't the case. Papa worked just as hard, if not harder, than everyone else. The way he worked made us want to work.

This sticks with me to this day. Even now, no matter what role I play on a team, one thing is consistent hard work. No matter if you're stronger than me, taller than me, faster than me, one thing you won't do is outwork me. That's all thanks to Papa.

People would pull into the station, and CJ and I would rush up to their cars, next to the self-service pump, and say, "I've got this! I've got this!" because we wanted to stack up those tips. I even learned how to change oil when I was still in elementary school, because Papa made it look so easy and we wanted to do everything he did. Seeing Papa run the company as both a boss and technician really opened my eyes and laid the foundation to strive for a hardworking reputation. If I think about how that translates into basketball, it resonates in focusing on defense, looking for any advantage, showing up first to the gym, and being the last to leave. These basic principles come from my days of grinding in the shop, trying to work as hard as my grandpa.

Jones Chevron had three bays and three gas pumps. There was the full-service pump where CJ and I hung out, trying to add enough tips to our stash to one day be able to buy our own Jordans, and then the self-service pumps, which was located closer to the street. Directly outside the service bays was a gathering place for some of Papa's longtime customers. A little group of old heads would set up shop on these two big old brown bus seats that Papa welded to the ground out front. This crew came to be known as the Jones Disciples. Talk about telling stories from way back: they had a million and one stories of how great it used to be back in the good ole days—and about 99 percent of them were definitely inappropriate for kids, but CJ and I didn't care, we were all ears, soaking up game as the guys said *whatever* came to mind.

If you've ever seen the movie *Barbershop* or have been in a Black barbershop, you know exactly the type of conversation I mean. These guys talked about everything under the sun and got real creative with their language. My folks didn't cuss at home, so CJ and I didn't either. We'd be pumping gas or wiping something down, and suddenly we'd hear, "And this mother#*$@*!" We'd look right up to try and hear what they were talking about. Usually, they were arguing about football or basketball, didn't matter if it was local high schools all the way up to the pros; they'd be praising Winston-Salem State one minute and MJ and the Bulls the next.

There was Mr. Kelam, Mr. Ulysses, and Mr. Mc-Coy who loved to come by and Mr. McCoy was always strolling up with his red cup in hand full of brown chunks of tobacco he'd spit out in between sentences. I almost just threw up writing that, it was so vile. There was also a Vietnam vet named Bo, who only had one arm. He'd take the left sleeve of his shirt and fold it up real nice and then place it into the pocket of his shirt so you almost didn't notice it. Bo will always have a special place in my heart. What I loved about him most was that he never wanted anyone to feel sorry for him. He wanted to prove to us that he could do anything a guy with two arms could do, so he'd lift up huge tires—never taking anyone's help. CJ and I would always ask him when he was getting his arm back. He didn't want us to feel bad, so he'd just tell us, "Oh, don't worry, I'm getting it back for Christmas." This was enough then to make us happy for him and we'd naively walk away until we'd ask him again next time. And then there was the most famous member of the Jones Disciples, Clarence "Big House" Gaines.

Now, if you're not from Tobacco Road or aren't a basketball fan, you might not know who that is, but in his day, for those in the know, Big House needed no introduction. He coached basketball at Winston-Salem State, an HBCU, for almost fifty years, becoming one of the winningest coaches in the history of college basketball; not just historically Black colleges and universities, but *all* of college basketball. He went on to be one of the few Black coaches to be inducted into the Basketball Hall of Fame. As a matter of fact, Big House Gaines is probably the most famous coach in the history of Black college basketball, and he would just come by and kick it out front with the rest of the Disciples. When Coach Gaines wasn't going on about Winston-Salem State, he loved to reminisce about his days in Baltimore, way back when he was a football star at Morgan State. Every time Big House would pull up to the bus seats out front, our young ears would open right up so we could take in all the stories about coaching, living in a different city, and being a big-time collegiate athlete.

As CJ and I started playing more sports, Big House would be curious, asking us about our games, how it was going, and who was doing what on the court. When we started getting more well known, we'd overhear him talking to Papa, saying, "I heard about your grandboys, especially the little one. I know the older one can play some ball, but they talking about the younger one being special."

One time he even came to watch me play. He made sure to find me after the game and said, "Hey, man, your little butt can play." It was one of the earliest moments I remember that the hopes and dreams of the NBA might not be that far away. The only reason why I got the chance to share that moment with Big House was because I was Jones's grandson.

On most days, Big House and the rest of the Jones Disciples, especially Mr. Ulysses, would sit around, drinking coffee, talking over each other, smoking cigarettes, and chopping it up. These guys loved to joke about Papa's dirty hands and fake teeth. Papa would snap back too, laughing so hard that we heard and saw those artificial Mr. Wilson– looking teeth bouncing around in his mouth. And Mr. Ulysses, being Mr. Ulysses, would never stop.

On most days, we'd order lunch from Ackingna's Place, a restaurant with a bright blue awning right down the road. I'd usually get some wings, CJ would get a burger, and Papa would get whatever he was feeling that day, usually a sandwich or some-thing that was easier to chew. We'd sit down getting ready to dig into lunch, with the Disciples usually eating with us too. Before he'd dig in, Papa, with his greasy-ass hands that probably just came off somebody's engine, would pop those hands right in his mouth and take his teeth out. The moment they came out, it looked like his whole face folded up. He'd plop them down right on the table, grab a little napkin, and wrap his teeth there while he ate. He'd try to say something, and his spit, the half-gummed-up food, and his words would get all mixed together.

"Jones, put your goddamn teeth back in your mouth before you try to talk!" someone would inevitably yell.

We all laughed, including Papa. I can't talk about Papa's teeth without mentioning that I swear he'd lose them every other day. It drove him and everybody else crazy. He'd just sometimes toss that napkin he wrapped his teeth in right in the trash by accident and then be digging through it later looking for them. If he didn't find them, he'd have to wait a couple of days to get a new set from the dentist. He'd just kind of go about his day without any teeth in his mouth until he had a new set.

When the guys weren't messing with each other, Mr. Ulysses would always find a way to keep the humor going. One of his favorites was his steering wheel joke.

Whenever, and I mean whenever, an old steering wheel was lying around, he would grab it, sneak into Papa's office, and say, "A customer just came in saying their steering wheel wasn't working right." Once he got Papa's attention, Ulysses would take the wheel, put it on his crotch, and start laughing, saying, "He said it was driving him nuts!" with a fluffy cloud of cigarette smoke surrounding his mouth. Even if there were no props available, he found a way to tell his old-fashioned crazy jokes.

It didn't matter if the shop was loud from laughter or dead quiet, Papa always had the AM radio playing in the background. Typical stuff kept going on repeat—news checks, traffic, weather, sports, whatever was happening locally, even some oldies but goodies would sneak into the rotation. But no matter what, Papa made sure that we heard the obituaries. They were read at the same time, every day, like clockwork. He'd be off working on a transmission, sneak a peek at the clock, and yell at one of us, "Hey, one of y'all, turn up that radio!"

We'd hear a little humming because these

speakers were way past their prime and the radio host would start reading off the names of everyone who had died in the last twenty-four hours. Papa would stop what he was doing, tell us all to quiet down, and listen to the names like it was a Sunday sermon. Maybe that's kinda creepy, but it was our normal.

"Aw, man, he passed" or "Oh no, not Mr. Such-and-such," Papa would say before taking his own personal moment of silence.

I swear he knew almost half the people who died and had a little story about most of them. I think he wanted us to know just a little bit about each person to honor their legacy, but part of me knew that he was talking mostly to himself, trying to make peace with another person he knew passing away.

"Oh no, I didn't know Gary was sick. That's so sad. He got ALL the girls back when we were in school. He had a mean Jheri curl and never stopped whispering in a girl's ear," Papa said of one of his old friends one day, before giving a little laugh, a nod, and then going back to work. He did this for everyone. I wasn't sure what was more impressive, how many people he knew in town or how much he remembered about every one of them. Papa's memory was not something to play with. I'm pretty sure that's where I get it from.

Sometimes Papa would get on us because we'd be out there with the Disciples, messing around, laughing at some of those dirty jokes, asking too many questions, and not doing enough work. He'd come over in his dark blue pants, light blue shirt, big red rag hanging out of his back pocket, trusty cigarette dangling as always, waving his hands like, "Shouldn't y'all be workin'?"

CJ and I would quickly get up as the Disciples finished smoking and chewing that tobacco, because we didn't want any problems with Papa. I should mention that having some kind of tobacco vice, whether it be cigarettes, cigars, or dip, was an unspoken rule of the Disciples. This was Tobacco Road after all, and everyone was smoking or dipping or chewing on something tobacco-related. I always knew that wasn't for me. In fact, I had a fear of tobacco. I saw Grandma Rachel pass away from lung cancer when I was eight, so

I always had it stuck in my head that smoking would kill you, in that weird way things affect you from when you were a kid.

We used to get so mad at Papa for smoking those cigarettes. Once, right after Grandma passed, CJ and I took his pack of Winstons and tore it up, breaking the cigarettes in half, and threw them all in the trash. We wanted to make a statement. We were kids, so we didn't realize how expensive cigarettes could be. Papa was big mad. He really let us have it in a way he never had before. "CJ! Chris! What did you do with my cigarettes?" We froze in fear. The last thing we wanted to do was be on Papa's bad side. "Y'all know how much cigarettes cost?! Y'all lost y'all damn minds?!"

We thought we were saving him from getting cancer and that we should be getting some type of award for helping him, for doing the right thing, but he didn't see it that way at all. Trust me, we never even thought about throwing his cigarettes away again. At least not like that. We switched it up on him instead and started taking them one by one when he wasn't looking so he didn't notice.

PAPA

We never judged Papa for smoking. Everyone in Winston-Salem smoked. I remember way back, when we took those drives to be dropped off at the service station and I decided to crack the car window to get some fresh air. The scent of tobacco would instantly creep in, overtaking our car, with the smell sometimes getting stuck into our clothes until we washed them. Back in the forties, 60 percent of workers in Winston-Salem were employed by the R. J. Reynolds Tobacco Company, which was founded about 150 years ago. Winston-Salem was once the largest city in North Carolina, with R. J. Reynolds being the second-largest tobacco company in America. For a long time, the Reynolds building was the tallest building south of Baltimore. It's hard to overstate how important Reynolds Tobacco had been to the way of life not just in Winston-Salem, but in the state of North Carolina—for those reasons, smoking, and all kinds of tobacco use, has been embedded in the culture, and was basically the heart of the city. Even my field trips in school were to the tobacco plant to see how cigarettes were made because that's what drove the local economy.

SIXTY-ONE

There were many times when people in the community, family or not, would head straight to the service station because they knew there would be work there for them. There were a couple of times when even my dad got laid off, and when that happened, he went to the service station and worked until he figured out his next move.

No one even considered just taking some time off if things didn't work out in your primary job, because Papa always had your back. The station meant grinding and doing what you were supposed to do for your family. Even before many of the guys who got laid off went home to share the news with their significant others, they'd hit Papa first, knowing he would at least try and find a way. And Papa welcomed them in with open arms and was ready to teach them a skill that would always be in demand—putting them in a position to take care of their families. No matter how many people were working there, one thing *fa sho* was that Papa always had to be the one to open and close the shop. And then, after he worked all day, he'd close down the station and come to our games. When he walked into

28

the gym, because of his hands, everybody knew where he was coming from.

It's because those hands truly represented his hard work, his labor, and the legacy he built for us. Sometimes I feel the same way about myself. I've had four hand surgeries. I've got the scars to prove it. At this point, my hands are evidence of the work I've put in and what my hands have helped me achieve on the court and in my career. They'll never be as grease-stained as Papa's, but they're for sure tested in their own way. I guess it's a bond we never knew we'd have. It's a little different, but it all means the same thing: HARD WORK!!!

3

RELENTLESS

- - - - - - - - - - - - - - - - - -

HOW YOU DO ANYTHING IS HOW YOU DO
EVERYTHING.
—MARTHA BECK

At this point, I don't know that I have a truly signa-
ture thing like Papa's hands, but I damn sure know
that we share our work ethic. Papa was relentless
in the garage, and I've taken that to the court. You
gotta be relentless. What else you gonna do?

I've always prided myself on doing the work.

That's who he was and who I believe I am. At the end of the day, people like Papa don't need to look flashy or require any kind of special attention outside of what a worker should get for the work they do. Papa didn't have ten service bays like one of those auto repair supercenters, but he had the ability to provide the highest level of service. I guess I knew I wasn't going to be seven feet tall, but I always figured that my work ethic could make up for anything I lacked in height.

Of course, I've always wanted to be explosive down the lane and dunk on everybody. Who wouldn't? But I learned from Papa to be scrappy, to use my perceived disadvantage as an advantage. How do I find the edge on guys without using physicality? I'm not necessarily tall for an NBA player, but I learned early on to be creative and to know how to pass, score, and win using whatever methods I could. I *think* the game. The energy I have now is the same energy I had in the backyard or at the YMCA playing with my boys, it's just on a different stage. I get that feeling now when I watch my fourteen-year-old son, Lil Chris, and my ten-year-old daughter, Camryn, play.

I always focus on doing the work because it makes you succeed in whatever you're trying to do. The work says way more about someone than all that meaningless talk, hype, or anything that only shines on the surface. Hard work is my preferred language, and I try to speak it fluently. I could talk about hard work day in and day out; it's all I know. Lord knows I hope that the results of that work show every time I step onto the court. Like for real, I will not stop. It's why I'm always saying, "Can't give up now." When I got traded from the Houston Rockets to the Oklahoma City Thunder, many people wrote me off. The first song I heard the next morning heading to my workout was a gospel song by Mary Mary called "Can't Give Up Now." The media gave us a 0.2 percent chance to make the playoffs that year. We ended up as the five seed and ironically lost to my old team, the Rockets, in seven games, but I never stopped believing in our team. I live by that song now and I write it on my shoes every game to this day.

Not giving up means having an edge. I quickly understood why the players who did all the little things were so important to teams. Sometimes guys are more concerned about what they look like than working hard, or become too focused on material things and completely forget about winning. For me, being a basketball player is not so I can have nice things and be well known; that all just comes along with it. What really drives me is the *grind*—how hard you have to work to perfect your game. The late nights, the early mornings. I truly love the game and I want to be the best at it. I proudly learned that from Papa, my mom and dad, and CJ. They molded and shaped me to be relentless in the pursuit of success, and in turn, I aim to do the same for my kids.

It can be a challenging balance sometimes to ensure that my kids appreciate the grind and earning the things that they have. One thing that being a parent made me realize is that my past is important in shaping their future. If I want them to value the process then they must know our family's history and how it taught me work ethic. This is why I feel it's so important that we continue to spend time in North Carolina to see where they came from.

My wife, Jada, their family, and I try to talk them through that now that they're a little older. Beyond the talking, and me telling them "back in the day" stories, I believed it was important to physically experience the energy at Papa's station. Smelling the air, inhaling the fumes, seeing where the pumps were, and just feeling East Winston. This would add a different layer to the values I try to teach my children. The service station was Papa's happy place.

"Y'all have to see Papa's service station. I don't even know what it looks like now, but we're going to take a trip back there soon, and I'll show you." I'd said that many times to Lil Chris and Cam.

It bothered me that we hadn't done that yet as a family. Sometimes my schedule makes it hard—a long season, travel, their school—but now they're at an age where we have to prioritize going home. They'll graduate high school before I know it and life is always just happening. I was crazy excited to show them the service station, and not just in a picture.

In the summer of 2021, there was finally a chance to do this. We were surprising my dad's parents with a home renovation. We took some time to show the kids the service station and where I grew up. I wanted them to understand and see why our family's roots are embedded in the soil of Winston-Salem.

Everyone is expected to work hard, starting with Papa, who opened his shop at seven in the morning every day. The world could be ending, but you could depend on that garage door sliding open right on time. Papa would even come in extra early on the days when CJ and I had basketball and football games so he could close up a little early to come and see us play; he tried to make sure he didn't miss us in action. Papa was an iron man who didn't take sick days, vacation time, or family leave for any reason. I still don't understand how he did it. Monday through Saturday, clock in, clock out, work. This didn't change until my grandma passed. My mom couldn't stand that he didn't take a break, but it was all he knew.

When my grandma Rachel died, it was my first experience with death so up close and personal. It's crazy talking about it now because of how it has affected me my entire life. Of course I didn't realize it at the time, I was just eight years old, but I still vividly remember when they closed her casket. We were sitting in the first row on the left side of my church, Dreamland Park Baptist Church. I was sitting right next to Papa and he put his arm around me and told me not to cry because I needed to be strong for my mom and Aunt Rhonda. Who knew that I would carry those words with me for the rest of my life? He had the strength to say those words to *me* in that moment when he had just lost his wife. That's the type of strength that only certain people possess.

As I looked over to the right, my aunt Rhonda was screaming at the casket in tears. The finality of death hit her, it hit us all. When that casket closed, it meant my grandmother was really gone. I've never gotten over that. I think that's why I have a hard time dealing with death and attending funerals to this day.

After Grandma's funeral, Papa finally gave in and decided to go on a cruise. He would try to do other stuff such as family gatherings and whatnot, but he always made up those missed hours at the station. Losing my grandma woke him up and allowed him to realize that he couldn't just work all the time. There was more to life than just working. I mean, he used to always stay open to 7:00 or 7:30 or later, but after our grandma passed, he made sure to close up by 6:00—which may not seem like a huge deal, but, to us, it was.

The hard work didn't begin with Papa; the DNA of our family's Winston-Salem roots goes as far back as chattel slavery. Peter Oliver, a skilled and ambitious potter and farmer, walked into a Pennsylvania courthouse in June of 1800 and demanded his freedom. The beauty of the story is that it wasn't a battle between him and a disgruntled slave owner; all of the Moravians worked together to secure his freedom. Oliver had figured out a way to trick the system, by selling his pottery until he earned enough money to pay a white man named Peter Lehnert to purchase him from his then owner. Oliver's owner probably thought that he had made enough money off his labor and then could turn a bigger profit by selling to Lehnert, and it worked like a charm. What the owner didn't know was that Lehnert and Oliver came up with this plan. As soon as Lehnert received Oliver, the two went to Pennsylvania to file for Oliver's freedom. This plan wasn't just done by two men, though; it was a group effort by the Moravians to help Peter pay for his freedom. The collective did it, not just Peter.

Once Oliver was free, he relocated back to Winston-Salem, where he married, had two children, continued to be a potter, and enjoyed his remaining days until he passed in 1810. Peter Oliver is my great-grandfather six times removed. I am so inspired by him, because he didn't come up with excuses; he created a plan and executed it, all based on hard work. Peter Oliver was relentless. My mother is currently working to have a park created in his honor and named after him in Winston-Salem. I truly believe that Peter planted the seeds that continued to be passed all the way down to Papa and eventually us.

When CJ and I started taking basketball more seriously, we couldn't put in the same time at the shop, but Papa didn't mind. He was just excited seeing us do our thing on the court. Looking back, it was such a big deal that Papa was willing to shut down his business a couple of hours early just to watch us play. I'm sure he lost money at times, but his priority—his family—was more important.

He took it down to the minute, though. You'd think someone doing that kind of work all day would want to go home, shower, change clothes. Not Papa. He didn't have any time to do all that. He'd walk right into the gym, work clothes on, grease everywhere. The only thing he changed was his shoes. He'd get rid of those black work boots and slip on some church loafers, as if that made a difference. Papa in his dirty uniform and shiny hard bottoms would slide to every game ready to cheer us on with a back pocket full of money. That cash was such a source of pride for him. One thing about Papa—he loved to make money, but helping people in the community with it was just as important to him.

I think he knew that people paid attention to him. He didn't put away every penny he made because it mattered to him that young kids would see a Black man with hard-earned cash. Those same kids who watched him earn were also able to watch him share with the community. He'd talk about the power of having your own money and how you had to work hard for it and earn it, and once you did, it was yours. His goal was to make sure we understood the value of a dollar.

Papa loved to be paid by his customers in cash. He accepted cards, and checks from some people for obvious reasons, but he loved cash. He used the cash to make change for customers, tip us, or buy whatever he wanted. For years, I sat back and watched him dig deep into his blue work pants and just peel through stacks of tens, twenties, and fifties like a human ATM before rolling it up and stuffing it back into his pocket.

I wanted to have cash like that.

It wasn't about the money itself for Papa, but the idea that money came from hard work and sacrifices. If that green paper was the by-product, then so be it, but the work that allowed him to provide for his family and help his community is what drove him.

I remember my first job outside of the gas station, when I was hired as an after-school counselor at Southwest Elementary School right next to my high school. I was beyond excited to get my first real paycheck—because Papa normally paid us in cash, and getting that envelope with my earnings all sealed up inside made me feel like I was grown as hell. My boss passed it to me, and I went outside and ripped open the envelope, only to be confused when I saw the amount. It was *way* less than I'd expected. This was my introduction to a little thing called tax deductions. The local government, the federal government, Social Security, and Medicare all took their cut at the same damn time! I was sick. Sick as hell. Papa never took taxes out of our checks, unless he was shorting us for some basketball shoes we wanted—which was a tax I was always glad to pay. But the check I got messed me up. I still cashed the check and folded the few measly twenties I received at the bank into a tiny roll. My little wad of cash was a joke compared to Papa's. Baby steps, though, baby steps.

My mom laughed when I went home that day hot about my check being short. She always ran the books and did the accounting for Papa and the service station. She knew just how bad tax deductions could be, and she knew the only way to learn that lesson is to learn it the hard way and see it for myself.

Everybody knew it was cool to have a pocketful of money, but Papa made it real, and more importantly, he made it exciting to earn it, on your own and for yourself. Entrepreneurship meant everything to him and put that same drive in me. The beauty of it is that he did it all with a smile on his face. Every time he opened the station, greeted a customer, he did it with a smile. Then he'd happily do it all over again the next day and the next day and so on. It's one thing to be forced to do hard work, but the vibe is completely different when the hard work makes you happy. That's why I credit Papa for giving me that mentality that I've strived for on the court—the ability to grind out from the opening tip until the final seconds of any game. It's about the work, being in the moment, laser focused on the task at hand. And it's about being willing to work harder for hard work's sake.

Because that is the job—and completing that job makes you relentless, like Papa. These teachings are what I'm trying to show Lil Chris and Cam by bringing them back to North Carolina and by showing them Jones Chevron.

4

GOING BACK

A MAN WITHOUT KNOWLEDGE OF HIMSELF AND
HIS HERITAGE IS LIKE A TREE WITHOUT ROOTS.
—DICK GREGORY

"Dad, is this it?" Lil Chris said as we pulled into what used to be the service station's parking lot. It's like I could smell the gas pumps all over again. My mind was instantly wrapped in nostalgia, with memories of me running in and out of this place when I was no bigger than Lil Chris—getting my tiny hands dirty, changing filters, and rotating tires flashed on repeat in my head. "Is this Papa's station?"

"It is," I answered, a little distracted. I took a deep breath. "It is."

My mind immediately raced back to the days when I spent so much time learning lessons that I would use forever, that helped me face some of the most difficult parts of my life. I felt the energy immediately. Teenage memories were on repeat, of me walking across the lot or playing on the same concrete with CJ, on the same corner, seeing the same trees off in the distance that haven't changed in twenty years—and might be there for a hundred more. It was almost like stepping out of a time machine. But it wasn't a time machine, because the JONES CHEVRON sign that Papa adored was long gone, and the building has been painted over multiple times—and the altar of cocoa-brown busted bus seats on which sat loyal customers is just a memory.

My wife, our kids, and the future of my family also flashed through my mind. Home. It was so nice to be home. Lil Chris and Camryn jumped from the car and began to look around. I followed them, looking at all the new people, the unfamiliar faces, the businesses that have popped up out of nowhere, and realizing how much Winston-Salem has changed.

Man, it felt good to be back. I hadn't stepped foot in this service station in a real long time. I was always on the move playing basketball, but I also wasn't rushing to revisit some of these places. There were some mixed emotions for a while. I wasn't ready, and even though the good outweighs the bad, there are still elements of trauma deep down that are tough for me to deal with.

As I saw Lil Chris, Cam, and Jada looking around, getting their bearings, and I heard them starting to ask some questions, my mind found ease in the good, as it usually does. Old stories I hadn't thought about in years emerged.

One of the coolest things to us as kids, before we could make tips from inspections, was knowing that because my granddad owned the station, we could pop the register and hit that change drawer at any time to take loose change for sodas, chips, candy, and other snacks—basically, whatever we wanted. In the second drawer on the left of Papa's desk was a huge black box full of change. CJ and I knew about that box, and that was a problem for only one person: my uncle Hubert, rest in peace. Our uncle Hubert, one of my grandfather's brothers, would always catch us going for that black box and say, "Y'all know you ain't supposed to be in that drawer!"

Of course, we'd play it off, "Oh yeah, yeah, Uncle Hubert. We was just making sure it's all there," or whatever excuse we could come up with. Then we'd slowly walk away, only to hit the box again later on, as soon as Hube was out of sight.

Other than Uncle Hubert and the Disciples, there were some real special characters at the service station who will live in my heart forever, like Happy.

"'Aye Chris!" I yelled over to my son. "Let me tell you about this guy named Happy."

"His mama named him that?" Lil Chris asked with a confused look.

"No, let me explain." I laughed.

Our official name for him was Happy, and that's what everyone still calls him to this day. We knew he "had seen some things" when he was fighting in Vietnam, so Papa always encouraged us to let certain things slide, and we did. Happy had perfect attendance at the service station, he was always around, and it didn't matter if it was a hundred degrees or below zero. Happy would be there, ready to help with any and everything.

We called him Happy because he laughed all the time, with an explosive, jittery chuckle that would allow you to see all thirty-two of his teeth, even those molars tucked all the way in the back. It didn't matter if we were depressed, angry, frustrated, or as happy as Happy, he would just bust out laughing. It was nice to have him around. When you were feeling down, his constant giggling and chuckling had a way of brightening your day. I remember hanging my head around the station after I had bad games, where I didn't play well, but I would see Happy and say, "What's up?"

"HAHAHAHAHAhaAAHHAHAhHaHAH!"

And then I would join in and laugh too, because why not? If Happy can be happy, then I can too. Together, the two of us, and usually CJ, would be laughing so hard but had no clue what we were laughing at. And suddenly, the bad game didn't seem so bad. When I got a little older, I found out that some terrible things had happened to Happy when he served our country in Vietnam. There was no talk of things like PTSD back then, and many Black soldiers like Happy didn't receive the aid, support, counseling, and love from that same government that they had fought hard to protect. They were expected to come home and resume life as if they hadn't seen fellow soldiers have their limbs blown off, witnessed mass murder, and buried dozens of their friends. The government failed to support Happy, so Papa was glad to step in, making Happy a fixture around the station.

Papa knew Happy just needed support but wanted to make sure we treated him like everyone else, even though we knew something was a little off. I thought about this a lot as president of the National Basketball Players Association, when we prioritized negotiating for better healthcare for retired NBA players. We needed to protect and support those that came before us, those that helped build the platform that we are part of now. Just like those players who came before us put the game in the great position it's in today, Happy gave us something and we needed to give him something back.

Generally, I wasn't raised to make exceptions for people or treat anyone differently, but in this case, Papa was the boss, and what he said goes. I later realized that though Papa was such a stickler for hard work, there was a reason Happy was the only exception. Papa had made it extra clear to us. It was a good exercise in being empathetic and meeting people where they are.

A few times I even went in to clean the bathroom and Happy would be in there sleeping. I'd run out and say, "Hey, Papa, Happy's taking a nap in the bathroom. I can't clean it right now."

If this were anyone else, Papa would be in there banging on the door, but with Happy, he would just pat me on the back and say, "Don't worry about it, Chris. Let him get some rest."

Things like this happened all the time at the station. Lessons were taught every day, not by telling, but by showing, which I think is one of the best ways to get things to stick. With this in mind, I wanted to give my kids a little history lesson about the neighborhood.

"Right now, where we are at is called East Winston. It's pretty much the Black side of town," I told them. "Papa took care of this community, and it took care of him. We didn't live over here, though; we lived on the other side of town that was mostly white."

Looking back, it was helpful for CJ and me to see the divide between Blacks and whites every single day right in our own backyard. This wasn't the first time we'd talked about race, of course, and we continue to educate our kids, especially in tough moments.

George Floyd's murder was obviously one of these tough moments. The day it happened, we were all sitting in the bathroom at our house in LA. I decided to show the entire video to Lil Chris and Cam. I know it sounds heavy but it was necessary. About halfway through the video, Cam began to cry. I thought she was crying because of what she was watching, which was partly true, but she was more so scared for her brother.

When I started talking, this was really when

Cam started crying. "Daddy, is this going to happen to Lil Chris?"

That crushed me. There are times as a parent where you just don't know what to say, and that was one of them. Of course, I consoled her and told her it wouldn't happen, that all of us were together as a family and loved each other. That went a long way, but I know in my heart that this is a real problem, and that I won't always be able to protect them as they grow older. Even with the life we have, a different life from where I came from and different from those of a lot of people growing up in Black America right now, our life is not immune to situations like this.

Back in 2020, the same year George Floyd was murdered, I was quarantining at home in LA. Once meetings started happening again, I was out driving to meet a business associate. Keep in mind here, at this point, I'd been in the NBA for fifteen years, six of them right here in LA, playing for the Clippers. My little cousin AJ was with me, and we were driving on the 405. I was driving, and AJ was sitting next to me. All of a sudden, we heard sirens go off; an LAPD officer was pulling us over. Now,

I'm rarely one to get too nervous, I can thrive in high-pressure situations, but you would not believe how hard my heart was beating as I guided the car off to the shoulder and saw a white cop step out of his patrol car and approach my window. I was scared to death.

Before he even got close, I did exactly what I thought I was supposed to do in these situations. I took my hands off the wheel and showed them to the cop. I kept them up in the air and even put them out the window just to be sure he saw them.

"License and registration?" he asked.

"Officer, I'm about to reach into the middle console." The moment I said that, I realized that he moved his right hand to his holster, so I said it again to be sure. "Officer, I'm telling you, I am about to reach inside this console and get my registration for you. Is that okay?"

I don't know why this upset him, but he got real mad. "Of course you can reach in there! Why are you even acting like that?" He started trippin' a bit and more forcefully telling me to show him my license and registration. It really seemed like he had no idea why I, a Black man getting pulled over by a white officer in 2020, would be a little hesitant and careful with what I was doing and what I was saying. Thank God this situation ended up okay, but I know it's not the last time CJ, AJ, Lil Chris, I, or millions of Black men in America today will be faced with something similar.

As much as people see me on TV wearing a jersey with my name on the back, as soon as I step out of that arena, I am no longer Chris Paul, the NBA player, I'm just another Black man like any other, especially to a white cop.

It's a good thing that a lot of kids may never truly understand the realities of the divide in this country, but it seeps in every now and then. Let me give you another example of how ingrained culture can be and trust me, I know little kids are innocent. We moved to a place where my daughter was the only Black girl in the class. Other young girls would talk about and touch her hair in fascination because she was the only one in her class with braids and the texture of hair she has. She didn't always understand why, but we had to explain to her that she was different and that's okay. Jada and I have the difficult task of teaching our kids the role race plays in our divided country, cities, neighborhoods, and schools.

Back at Papa's station, we continued to explore our family history. We had done this same trip in Jada's neighborhood years earlier. "You need to know your roots," Jada chimed in.

Cam and Lil Chris walked around, slowly examining the walls, the register, the chairs, imagining what the place was like back in the summers when I'd worked there daily.

"What'd you guys do all day, Dad?" Cam asked.

"There were no iPads, baby, and we didn't spend all day with our face in a screen," I told them both, watching their eyes spread in amazement. "You worked and figured out how to have fun without the crutch of technology."

The kids laughed, but I let them know that I was serious. We couldn't watch TV or play PlayStation all day. CJ and I went outside to play. We just played anything to make the time go by, we just figured it out. In the beginning, CJ would win like he always did back then, but that competitive edge was real.

So real that sometimes we didn't even finish a game because we were fighting so much. We fought about everything, all the time. Everything was a competition, even who got to sit in the front seat on a drive with Mom or Dad. We'd go as far as sitting in the car an hour before a ride because you did what you had to do. If you wanted the front seat, you had to get there first. Losing to CJ at anything, big or small, constantly pushed me to always try to be better. No matter what we were playing, he forced me to get the hang of things really quickly and earn my own wins. Solitaire on Papa's computer was the closest thing we had to a daily video game, but we didn't care for that—we were too busy living, creating our own fun. And when we weren't making that fun, we were working or learning another thing Papa taught us over and over, especially as we got older: becoming self-sufficient.

I know this is a different world we all live in now, but I cringe when I think about how sometimes technology and access make it more challenging for my kids to learn those lessons as easily. I see all the tools they have in their classrooms. I also know how many classrooms and school districts lack that kind of support. That kind of education should be available for everyone, so one of the biggest missions in my foundation, the Chris Paul Family Foundation, is leveling the playing field and making sure all schools have access to the same technology and learning tools. This is why Jada and I make a point to take trips like this when we can and have them seeing, feeling, and experiencing the world, not just their bubble. It's crazy that by exposing us to everyone in the shop, this is what Papa did for us. And we don't water those lessons down, just like he never did. Papa spoke to us like we were his peers; he gave us real advice that we can apply in real time.

"I don't ever want to have to answer to anyone! Especially a white man," Papa would sometimes say, reminiscing on the days he worked himself to the bone at the milk company or for the landlord he had at Jones Gulf before he owned his shop. "Nobody owns me. I'm my own boss. A white man is not going to tell me where to go, when to be there, how to dress, or what to do. That's for damn sure."

Everybody brags about being their own boss now, but Papa was hip to it a long time ago. He owned his own business in a time when many Black bosses did not exist. He was born in 1941, seventy-six years after slavery allegedly ended in 1865. He, like Black Americans today, really felt the inequality. He knew he was going to change the status quo and having complete control was not common for Black people at that time. He was a pioneer and we celebrate him for that. By being in charge, Papa was also in the position to make sure that all the people around him were making their fair share of money as well. And it was such a family business. Both of my parents benefitted from his example of being hardworking, successful in their own careers, and putting in hours at the shop.

My dad worked at Aigis Mechtronics, where he oversaw the robotics assembly line. This was way back when robotics had first come out. He started as a machine operator and continued to get promotions because he's a quick learner. Before you knew it, he was teaching other people how to do it and running the whole assembly line.

While my dad was working at Aigis, Papa had reached out to him because as times were changing and more things were going digital, Papa needed someone to learn how to input the state inspections data and emissions tests that were now required to go into a computer. My dad agreed, of course, so he was now spending a bit more time around the station even though he had a full-time job and his hands were full being a husband to our mother and a father to us.

Papa saw this as an opportunity. While at the shop, he taught my dad how to change brake pads. He believed that changing brakes and doing other things on cars would be easy for my father because he already knew so much about robots. He was right. Dad would be working at Aigis, and a co-worker would approach his desk like, "Hey, Charles, my money is funny right now, but I need some new brakes. Can you help me out?"

My dad would go right outside on his lunch break and knock it out.

Fixing brakes is actually a lot simpler than it seems—I still remember how to do it to this day. So, my dad would gather up the necessary tools from his car before getting started. He would need some mechanic's gloves so his hands wouldn't be permanently stained like Papa's, a lug wrench, a nut remover, a jack, a jack stand, a plastic tie, a C-clamp, the new brake pads, a can of brake fluid, and a baster used for drawing out any overflowing brake fluid.

I now imagine my dad carrying these items over to his coworker's car, assessing the vehicle, cracking the door open, and then pressing down the emergency brake, which is very important. Papa always said, "Never, ever forget to make sure that emergency brake is down. If you don't, you are going to be in a world of trouble!"

Before you prop the car up with the jack, you want to take the nut remover and loosen each nut—trust me, it's a lot easier while the car is on the ground, as the weight gives you more leverage. After that, you can prop the car up and get to work by taking the nuts completely off, removing the wheel, and then the slider bolt.

Identify the caliper, which is the part of your disc brake system that houses your pads and pistons—you'll see it on the side, and you need to pivot it up, so that you can slide out the old pads and retract the pistons. Check your brake fluid level; if it's too low, add a little, but don't top it off, because the fluid level naturally goes down as the pads wear;

if it's too high, use the baster to take some out, because you don't want it to overflow. Pop the new pads in and reposition that caliper. Put your slider bolt back in, put your tire back on, and tighten the nuts after lowering the jack. Do the exact same thing on the other side, collect your money, and you'll be good to go. The whole process takes about an hour—forty minutes if you were as good as my dad and Papa.

My dad took advantage of the situation and was able to pull in money from the set of skills he learned from Papa and apply them at his nine-to-five. The best part about it is that my dad loved working on cars as much as he loved helping people, so it was a win-win—as a matter of fact, my dad still could change the brakes if he needed to. Y'all don't get it. My dad really loves cars.

My mother worked at Wachovia Bank as a lead tech analyst. Back when Mom was in high school, she had gained acceptance into what was called the co-op program, which allowed talented students to attend classes for half the day and work for the other half. Many students had the opportunity to start their jobs at 1:00 p.m., but my mother's bank job didn't begin until 5:00 p.m., so she had a little extra time every day for her studies. Numbers always came easy to my mom; fractions, equations, and all kinds of theories danced around in her head before she scribbled them into her notebook, always solving the problem. Mom was like a human calculator, which made her stay in that program until she graduated from high school.

My mom ended up being so good that the bank offered her a full-time position the day after she graduated. She had to make the decision between going away to college or taking the job at Wachovia. This wasn't a difficult choice, because she had fallen in love with my dad and had no plans to leave Winston-Salem.

Over the years, my mom continued to advance at Wachovia, working her way up to the position of a managing tech analyst. My mother used all the skills she learned at the bank to take care of all of Jones Chevron's accounting needs—by managing everything for Papa, controlling the books, and making sure everyone and every bill was paid on time. Everybody worked all the time—we're relentless, remember? As the oldest child of his, she was a driving force behind Jones Chevron, and it was amazing to watch.

When we were really young, Granny, my dad's mom, would also drop us off at Papa's on the days she had to work. This taught us that the grind was real on both sides of our family. Granny would be up early getting to her job, and when we pulled up at 6:30 a.m., Papa was already dressed in his jumpsuit, ready to get cracking. We'd usually have a little breakfast first that Mama packed for us, a sip of that sugary coffee, but as soon as we finished, we both went after the red rag.

The red rag was everything, and you couldn't do anything without it. You had to put the red rag in your pocket before you turned on the pumps, turned on the lights, or refilled the gas that was in the ground. Papa helped us mature a lot earlier than most kids. When we got a little older, even though we didn't have driver's licenses, Papa let us move the cars around on the lot of the service station. This was my first unofficial driver's lesson—and I enjoyed whipping everything from big Cadillacs to old Oldsmobiles around the lot. We constantly worked, and we loved it—from that first sip of coffee in the morning, to the fatback sandwich from Ackingna's we enjoyed for lunch, we worked.

"We got it! We got it! It's hot out here. Let us take care of that for ya," CJ and I would say, with messy faces having just drunk some Welch's grape soda, as we'd catch customers coming toward that full-service pump. We'd try to guide them away from the self-service ones so that we could pump their gas with a smile, thinking of the tip we'd get off them. Do that enough times over a summer, we'd have enough money for some nice sneakers, maybe even a pair of Jordans, come the first day of school.

Work was actually fun. Not to get too spiritual, but as the Buddha says, "You should be able to see a person work, and play, and not be able to tell the difference." That's what we had at the service station, the opportunity to play all day and get paid.

I stood outside what used to be Papa's station, remembering all this, when I heard a voice.

"Yo, Chris! Chris?" an excited, raspy voice howled. "Chris Paul? Is that you?"

I looked up and squinted my eyes, focused on the familiar silhouette coming over my way. At first glance, I couldn't tell who it was, but I soon realized it was a familiar face I hadn't seen in so long. That's the way it is when you're at home.

Once we got done talking, both of my kids had a thousand questions apiece. "How many cars used to come through here?" "Did you ever see cars smashed up from getting hit?" "How did Papa learn how to do all this stuff?" "Did you wash the cars too, like they do here now?" There were so many more, they were rapid-firing questions the way only kids can. I was eager to answer them all, but first I had to give them the official lay of the land, because a lot had changed since the gas station belonged to my family.

For starters, the gas pumps were gone. The building operates as a car wash now. We loved those gas pumps because Papa didn't make the family pay for gas—it was a perk of the job.

Most normal everyday working people are not used to free gas. My family, we didn't know what it felt like to swipe our cards at a gas pump, because Papa owned the station. Both sides of my family went to Dreamland Park Baptist Church, and it would have made sense economically and environmentally for us to carpool, but we didn't—as a matter of fact, we all rode solo with big smiles on our faces, because we knew Sunday was free gas day in our family. Some of our family members—the generous ones—would even try to pay Papa, but he wouldn't have it. Everyone would just pull up to the service station right after the pastor gave the benediction and church let out, men still in our suits and ties, the women still in their beautiful hats and well-crafted dresses, and we would all graciously fill up our tanks.

"So Papa could afford to just give the gas away?" Lil Chris asked.

"Only to family," I responded. "Giving it to everyone for free would be bad business."

Back in the day, gas was only a dollar—but it wouldn't have mattered if it were five dollars, because we got it free. Sometimes friends of mine—or friends of CJ's—would say, "Hey, can we swing past the gas station—you know, to fill our tanks up?"

"Oh, sure, you could come by," we'd say and

laugh. "But you ain't getting it for free." Every now and then he'd let me bring a homie or two by but it wasn't all the time.

Once the kids and Jada and I had walked around the outside enough, I swear I saw some of the same weeds sneaking through the sidewalk all these years later, even with all the other changes the new owners had made. We kept going and went inside the service station. It had undergone a series of changes too. Imagine walking into your old childhood home and feeling like the rooms had shrunk—everything was rearranged, misplaced, or simply damaged. I shook off the feeling of déjà vu as I walked in there and attempted to quiet my mind. I had been guilty of going into my head since we'd hopped out of the car, but I wanted to remind myself that this wasn't really about me reminiscing on how the shop used to be, but about Lil Chris and Cam getting the opportunity to experience a huge piece of their history.

"So the desk was over there, and your uncle CJ and I would post up over there for breaks or in between completing whatever task Papa gave us that day," I said as I pointed to different sections of the room. "We had a soda machine—it sat right there—and whenever we made some extra change, we'd blow it on grape soda or Dr. Pepper."

Lil Chris and Cam were taking this in. I could tell they were getting a little bored by Jada and me doing this, but it was important, and they knew that. I think they also saw how comfortable I felt around the station, even all these years later. I was happy, but, as I said, we faced some hardships here too.

Beyond some of the trauma that I still deal with when thinking about Jones Chevron, some of the jobs Papa would give us were also frightening. Cleaning the bathroom comes to mind. Imagine scrubbing up after a guy who couldn't find the toilet in a small bathroom smellier than a pile of shit. That was the job, so I did it. Not happily, but I did it. And I kept that attitude throughout my playing career. Sometimes it's pretty, and sometimes it's doing the dirty work that no one wants to do, anything to help the team win—even if it means scrubbing a nasty-ass bathroom.

Changing tires made up for that. I love changing tires. I'd walk up on the car, hike up my jeans, get down on my knee, and rotate as many wheels as Papa told me to. On some of those days, my hands would look like small, dirty versions of his. I would go off and try to scrub them clean with the same soap Papa used. The only difference is that it worked for me, but I can't say the same for Papa. Every time I saw some grease on my palms or under my nails, I got excited because I knew I was getting a little closer to my hands looking like Papa's.

I also enjoyed performing oil changes, a skill I still have to this very day. The habit of buying a new car and checking the oil, or the fact that it takes six bottles to fill an oil pan, will never leave me. I'm proud of my service station roots and the fact that I can rotate tires and change oil with the best of them.

We really bonded with Papa over those summers, spending a ton of time together—from early in the morning when we arrived, to the beautifully delicate process of setting up, and then grinding until it was pitch-black outside. I loved it and, believe it or not, I miss it. And maybe that's another part that I wanted for Cam and Lil Chris, not necessarily to learn how to change oil and rotate tires, but to pick up skills and values from home, from our family—skills that they can use on their journey, and maybe even share with their own kids someday.

"I'm good on fixing cars, Dad," Lil Chris joked.

"You think you are until you go on a long road trip with your future wife and you don't have the first clue how to change your flat tire."

While continuing our tour, I started to really think about Lil Chris's and Cam's futures. The feeling of being back home, in the shop, and the influx of the countless childhood memories CJ and I learned from made me wonder if I was spoiling them too much. I want the best for them, they deserve it, but where do you draw the line? I'm sure I'm not the only parent who struggles with this.

Lil Chris and Cam have a lot, but Jada and I are constantly trying to make sure they appreciate the little things and work hard on that. CJ and I didn't do everything around the house, but at least we had to fold the clothes and clean our room, and if we didn't do those things, we definitely would be in trouble—with both Mom and Dad. It was our responsibility, and we learned from it. We try to instill this same work ethic in Cam and Lil Chris. It's not exactly the same, but you'd better believe they have a list of chores they have to do before they can do anything else they might want to be doing. They get them done too. We limit iPads and video games to just the weekend, and only if they do all their chores the week before. There's so much to learn from giving kids responsibilities and instilling that work ethic in them, like my parents and Papa did for CJ and me.

The kind of life that my children enjoy is very different from what we defined as luxury growing up—namely, Jordans. I've been part of the Jordan family for so long, we have an insane amount of Js around our house. It's crazy to put that into perspective, even for my son, because Jordans used to mean something totally different from boxes that just show up at the house whenever we want them. We're blessed. We're better than blessed. Growing up, we not only valued Air Jordans for the style, we valued them because we had to work for them. We could look at our shoes and physically see the work.

For CJ and me, like any young Black kids in the '90s, Jordans were it, you had to have them—end of story. Back when I was in sixth grade, the Jordan 13s were *it*. The ones that Denzel rocked in *He Got Game* had dropped. I earned the money to buy them, getting hands dirty, working at the station, it was only right. You should have seen me chasing down people, boxing CJ out, and making sure I got every full-service fill-up to add to my tip jar. Finally, when I had enough cash saved up, I went to Foot Locker to buy them.

I skipped the black-and-white pair and settled on a navy blue pair, with the hologram on the side. The first time I cracked the box, the smell of success, made up of fresh leather and crinkly wrapping paper, brushed against my nose. They were perfect, I did not want to take them off, but I was too smart to wear them in gym class. I still remember getting changed for gym that day. All the other students were just watching my feet as I slowly pulled the shoes off and carefully placed them in my locker. Like I said, I wasn't crazy enough to scuff up my new Js in gym class. I'd be a crazy person to run around in those Jordans, and nobody was crazy enough to steal them, at least I thought.

We hooped in gym, and I did what I normally

did on the court, hit some jumpers and worked on my game, the usual, while thinking about my shoes the whole time. When the bell rang, I jetted down to my locker, only to see it flung open and my belongings scattered.

"Who was near my locker?!" I yelled to anyone brave enough to come near me. "Where are my shoes?! Y'all got me all the way messed up!"

My brand-new, navy blue, barely worn Jordans were stolen right out of my locker. To make matters worse, I had to wear my regular-ass gym shoes for the rest of the day and then go home and face my dad.

"Why would you leave those expensive shoes alone?!" my dad yelled after he heard what happened.

"I put my lock on, Dad," I said.

"You know people break locks all the time," my dad said angrily. "Maybe you need to be punished for being careless."

"But, Dad—"

My father cut me off with wide, furious eyes, and I knew to shut my mouth, even though I thought it was silly to punish me for having my shoes stolen;

after all, I was the victim. My Js were gone. Mom and Dad were hot about that, but it didn't make much sense to me at the time. Someone stole my shoes that I saved up for and bought, and I had to suffer for that? We had put so much weight on that one pair of shoes, and it puts it all in perspective for me now.

I know it's on Jada and me to instill the value of hard work in our kids because they're not growing up working at the service station, or cutting grass in one-hundred-degree weather, but we are teaching them the same values in different ways. We work hard to teach them that same self-sufficiency that Papa taught us.

As we were wrapping up and heading back to the car, I saw Lil Chris checking out the neighborhood—the lack of resources and seeing things like worn-down cars that looked very different from the ones in the neighborhood we're accustomed to now. I imagined that this reality seemed impossible to him, that he couldn't believe people lived like this and that his family came from here. He could only compare it to his reality and the many privileges that the game of basketball has afforded our family. That's why this trip was so important to us. Showing the kids perspective and having them understand the importance of hard work had really sunk in. You can only appreciate where you're going if you know where you've come from.

Lil Chris looked around. "Dang, Dad, I can't believe this is where you grew up."

"I love it here. It's just different. That's all."

One of my group chats is made up of my homies that I grew up with, many of whom still live in the area, and they always keep me up to date on what's happening. One of them posted a video of a fight that broke at Hanes Mall back in Winston-Salem one night. I pressed Play and witnessed a group of young Black boys, probably all from different parts of Winston-Salem, chaotically throwing punches at each other until one pulled out a gun and broke apart the crowd with shots. "It's like someone gets killed every week," another friend responded. This kind of stuff happens not just here but everywhere. I think about this when trying to toe the line of educating and preparing my kids but not scaring them.

With Papa, working hard was about giving yourself choices. If you have means, you can make choices about things you want and things you want to do. When it comes to my kids, it's hard because your choices don't mean as much when you have all the options in the world. It's easy to instill being relentless in a kid when you can't afford to mess up. If I was going to make it to the NBA, I had no margin for error. And knowing that forced me to not take anything for granted.

We all smiled as we pulled out of the lot of the service station. As we did, I put my hand on Jada's knee. We gazed out at those streets I had seen for the millionth time, finally with our kids here with us to share the experience, and it felt like we were seeing everything we knew with a fresh perspective. It also had me remembering when Jada and I first got together.

Let me tell you a bit about the foundation and most important part of our family, my wife, Jada Paul. She laughs at me, because one thing she always tells me is how I'm too hard on Lil Chris, but I literally will do anything Cam asks me to do. I'm a girl dad, what can I say? Jada knows this all too well because she has the same effect on me. Always has and always will. It's been that way ever since the first time I laid eyes on her in the LJVM Coliseum.

Funny enough, I met one of Jada's friends at church prior to that and she thought that we would be a good match. She said something to me about how I should call Jada but I didn't really pay it no mind. I never had to call a girl. (Don't tell her I said that.) So, even though I had heard about her prior, Jada and I actually first met at the Frank Spencer Holiday Classic. Our high school rivals were playing in the championship against one another. After my school won (which I obviously must mention), we were standing on the stairs before leaving and that same friend of hers just put it on the table: "Why you ain't call my friend yet?" What she didn't realize was I thought Jada should have been trying to call me.

After meeting at that tournament, I saw her friend was probably right to try and set us up, so I decided to finally call her. What really attracted me to Jada was the fact that she was so real, and she loved that I was so driven for our age. As you can probably guess, by this time, everyone loved what I could do on the basketball court. I was used to that kind of praise. But she was excited, as she says, that I was a good person because of where I came from and my ability to show affection. I credit my parents and Papa with that. Although I was a McDonald's All-American, I didn't go to college knowing I would wind up in the NBA. I went to Wake Forest to get a great education and finished my communications degree at Winston-Salem University as I wanted to finish at an HBCU.

When we met, Jada was a sophomore at UNC Charlotte, about an hour or so south of Wake Forest and Winston-Salem, but when she was not in class, she spent most of her time at Wake with me. Her presence made everything around me easy, like an escape from the anxiety and pressures that come with being a Division I college basketball player. I felt like she instantly understood me because she was from the same area as my family and me. After a few months of dating, I had become so connected to Jada that I wanted to take the next big step and really introduce her to my family. This had the potential to get real ugly real fast, LOL. Like they say, one small step for man, one giant leap for mankind.

Now remember I was the baby boy, so my mom wasn't too crazy about any girl getting close to me. As a matter of fact, I tried to bring a girl home to my parents once and it didn't go over too well. And I had never brought a girl around my entire family. That alone let Jada know how serious I was about our relationship. I imagine Jada was nervous as hell that day. I know I was, but she's the one who had to go sit in the stands with fifty of my family members while they all watched me play. Unfortunately, I didn't even get to introduce her myself because I had to get ready for the game so she was really getting tested. It's crazy to think back that long ago, two kids and eleven years of marriage later. Her family, my family—now it's all one big happy family. When it comes to Jada's family, her parents have always treated me like the son they never had.

After a few years of dating, I got a phone call from Jada that she was pregnant with Lil Chris. It was the happiest I've ever been in my life, but I'll never forget how scared I was to tell my parents. This wasn't ideal by Southern Baptist church standards, but it was our story and I'm a firm believer that everything happens for a reason. Becoming parents and growing together, I knew I wanted to spend the rest of my life with Jada, so a year after Lil Chris was born, I proposed.

In order for her not to find out what I had planned, I had to do a whole lot of sneaking around to create the perfect memory for us. The most difficult part was the planning process because Jada is not the easiest person to surprise, but I was up for the challenge. Jada had spent so much time with me during our college years, especially at Wake, that I thought the perfect place for us to get engaged would be at LJVM Coliscum, the site of the Frank Spencer Holiday Classic where we first met.

This wasn't going to be one of those typical Jumbotron engagements; I had to think more creatively. First and foremost, I asked her dad for permission to take her hand in marriage. Next, I went out, bought a ring, and recruited my assistant coach at Wake, Jeff Battle, to help me out. His job was easy. All he had to do was answer the phone and act like I was coming to talk to the team and join their meeting.

As we got close, I pulled out my phone. "On my way to the meeting now, Coach B. I'm almost there," I said into the phone.

We pulled into the back of the Coliseum, and I thought Jada started to suspect something, because a curious look came over her face. She was confused why the team would be meeting in the off-season and why they'd be meeting so late at night. Neither of those things made sense.

"Where are all the cars?" she asked.

"Well, maybe everyone parked in the front," I replied anxiously. We entered the arena.

"Where are we going?"

"The locker room," I said, trying to reassure her. We walked through the locker room. No one was in there.

"Where is everyone?" she asked.

"Oh, they must be out on the court." At this point, I knew she'd probably figured out that something was up, but it was almost time. I just had to keep throwing her off a little longer.

"Just follow me," I continued. We kept walking

and finally got to the steps where we first met. When she cocked her head and fixed her lips to ask another question about what the hell we were doing there, I quickly spun around and got down on one knee and told her that I wanted to be with her for the rest of our lives. I asked her if she felt the same and if she'd do me the honor of being my wife. She happily said yes. Well, first she burst into tears and I lost her for a minute, but then she said yes.

I was thinking back on that moment as we drove through Winston. I fixed the mirror and looked in the back seat. We now have these two beautiful kids and are charged with the task of making sure they are receiving everything they need, emotionally, spiritually, mentally, and financially. And I know for certain, I wouldn't want anyone else on this ride with me.

5

THE GAME

Parkland High School, Winston-Salem
Parkland vs. West Forsyth High
November 20, 2002

There was a sticky fog that sealed the gym airtight—fans and onlookers finding their seats on the bleachers didn't make it any better. It was the first game of my senior year. I was in my head searching for quiet, for peace. The kind of quiet to focus amid noise and chaos, but I was having a hard time.

My mom and my aunt Rhonda had both attended Parkland High School, which made tonight's game even more emotionally charged. We'd normally talk junk to each other when our schools matched up but this wasn't that kind of night.

"Tonight, I'm playing for Papa," I told David Gelatt, my backcourt mate whom I usually called DG. "That's all I'm worried about right now. Tonight is for Papa."

"Of course, bro," DG said, shooting me a nod in agreement.

My entire family was in the stands, everyone except Papa. It was the first game of the season that he had missed. I was sick to my stomach looking over at the crowd and not seeing those big, square frames sitting on top of his wide, comforting smile.

"You good, Chris?" one of my teammates asked. I nodded, thinking that I was as good as anyone in my situation could be.

My teammates knew what was happening with my family and me—and that I was going through something that seventeen-year-olds shouldn't have to go through, that nobody should have to go through. Something that most people couldn't understand, even if they try their hardest—so other than the occasional *you good?*, they left me alone.

At the same time, basketball was booming for me. My seventeen-and-under AAU team had won the championship, which led to me starting to get some national attention. I signed to Wake Forest and made the McDonald's All-American team. But none of that mattered at all now compared to what was going on with my family. My best friend wasn't there.

My coach, David Laton, approached me during warm-ups. "How you feeling?"

"I'm good, Coach," I said, trying to brush the anxiety off and get a shot up.

"Chris, I'm serious," Coach said in a deeply concerned tone. "Tell me how you feel."

"Listen, if we get a lead tonight," I said, looking over my shoulder, "please let me play."

"No problem."

Normally, when we were blowing teams out by twenty or thirty, Coach would put me on the bench to let some of my teammates get some minutes.

"You ready?" DG asked. I nodded as I took my place on the court.

The game tipped, we quickly began moving through our offense, that anxiety completely faded, and I started scoring.

And scoring.

And scoring.

And scoring.

Three-pointers, midrange, step-backs, dunks—everything was going in. I felt unstoppable. I couldn't miss if I tried. The other team tried to double me, triple me, rotate defenders to me, but it didn't matter, they couldn't stop me from scoring.

My teammates were going crazy. "Keep going, C! Keep going!"

We all knew the North Carolina state record for points scored in a single game was sixty-seven and was held by a guy with the initials MJ Michael Jordan was special to us North Carolina kids, having played his high school ball at Laney, just a few hours down I-40 in Wilmington. But it wasn't about the record for me, and I wasn't even thinking about stats or passing MJ—my energy, my heart, and this performance felt spiritual. In the moment, I had felt something higher that filled me as I watched the rim grow bigger and bigger and bigger, with more and more of my shots falling in.

I wished Papa was in the building so bad, I could almost feel him there, but in actuality I physically needed him there.

6

DREAMLAND

- - - - - - - - - - - - - - - - -

MAKE SURE YOU HAVE LOVE TO SHARE,
HEALTH TO SPARE, AND FRIENDS THAT CARE.
—QUINCY JONES

I feel so fortunate and blessed, because honestly, I feel like I have the best family in the world. No, we are not perfect by any means and have our fair share of issues like any other family; however, my family always took care of me, with or without basketball. They never hesitated to show or stress the importance of unconditional love. That is our family story: unconditional love. And that story started at Dreamland Park Baptist Church.

My mother always had great admiration for her hardworking father. Papa wasn't just known as a hard worker by the people in my family; the whole community knew he worked from seven to seven. My grandma Rachel would pick up my mom, Robin, every day from school, swing her past the service station to visit Papa and his cast of employees, and then go home to prepare dinner. This routine occurred six days a week—except on Sundays, the day my mom's family would attend Dreamland.

My bloodline runs back generations in Dreamland, on both sides. Dreamland Park Baptist was the only place where Papa could relax and actually sit down. I know my mom and grandma were happy to see him do so. Everything my mother learned about the Bible and building her relationship with God originated at Dreamland, and it's the place where she met a guy named Charles Paul, my dad.

My dad's family is from East Winston. His neighborhood was similar to Belview, where Mom was raised—with most of the residents being employed by R. J. Reynolds or Western Electric. Respect was extremely important on both sides of my family and they instilled that in me at an early age.

My dad taught me to honor and revere my elders always—as a matter of fact, he taught me to be respectful to anyone and everyone. He'd make sure I'd walk into a room and acknowledge everyone, shaking their hands and making eye contact. It's how I was raised; it's a Southern thing, which may seem small, but is our way of showing respect.

I would be in the house, and my mom would yell out, "Chris!" and I'd respond, "Yes," and my dad would pop up out of nowhere like, "What did you say?" And then I would quickly change it to "Yes, ma'am," because that's the only appropriate way to respond. My dad is an old-school Southern man who put the fear of God in me and my brother. He taught us right from wrong and made sure we kept our heads on straight and always surrounded us with the right people. My dad raised us with manners that I am proud to pass on to my kids.

Now when I tell you that Dreamland is a tight-knit community, I mean Dreamland Baptist is *really* a tight-knit community—so tight that my mom's parents and dad's parents were actually best friends. They did a lot of things together: dinners, card games, whatever it was, they were always together. My dad played football at East Forsyth and would swing by to check on his younger siblings after he graduated. It was then that he and my mom started dating.

Initially, my dad didn't even think about dating my mom because he thought she was too spoiled. And he was right to a certain extent. My mom and my aunt were Papa's only daughters and the spoiled little princesses of Jones Chevron. My dad felt like my mom would run him ragged and he wanted no part of that mission. But as we all know, you can plan all day, but you can't control destiny. What's meant to be will be, and the two of them eventually fell in love and got engaged.

We have a really big family on both sides—too many people to even fit inside the church—so those two lovebirds had to move to a bigger venue, Masonic Temple, to house their ceremony. After the big wedding, they started their journey, and began to make their own family traditions. They bought their first home together in Lewisville, right outside of Winston-Salem.

There was an older gentleman my dad was friends with who came past the service station while my dad was working there. He noticed that my dad owned a little sports car that he had to put brand-new tires on every year. One day, this friend pulled my dad to the side and said, "Hey, young man, why don't you have a house? You should have a house."

My dad, young and full of energy, shrugged. "I can't afford a house."

"You don't think so?" the older gentleman said. "If you can afford that car and them wheels you put on it, then you can afford a house." He went on to explain to my dad how to go about getting a house with the money that he was making. My dad followed all his instructions and sure enough, my parents got the house.

The house my folks finally bought was at 801 Lewisville Clemmons Road, a redbrick home with green shutters that sat on the corner. We had a front yard, a backyard, and a huge satellite dish that sat in our yard. Huge satellite dishes were extremely popular around this time; everybody had them. For one Christmas, my dad bought us a go-kart, and since I was the little brother, I was in the passenger seat when CJ whipped around the corner, threw me out next to the satellite dish, and then crashed into the picnic table. That was his typical big-brother behavior back then.

At the end of our driveway was a one-car garage, and if you walked into it, you walked right into the basement, which was also a den area that my dad renovated. Initially, it was nothing but a concrete space where CJ and I used to work on ball handling, baseball, whatever we could do with a ball without pissing off my folks too much. One year, my dad got a bonus and had it redone with some actual flooring, carpet, couches, and speakers. I had to clean the den every Saturday morning with some Pine-Sol and a red rag from the service station. We were so excited about it, this became the new hangout for us and our friends.

If you ran through the front door, my parents' bedroom was on the left and the living room was on the right, then you'd hit the kitchen. So, CJ and I could never sneak around and do anything slick because all roads led to Mom and Dad. Even when I was in college, one time when Jada stayed over, my parents made her sleep upstairs, and I had to sleep downstairs. They weren't going for any funny business, LOL. I couldn't even sneak up to her because I would have to pass their room, and they would have for sure heard that squeaky floor and those squeaky doors. That house was creaking and cracking all the time. To me, I was a grown man at that point, but they still weren't having it. That's real life!

It wasn't just the layout of the house that gave us trouble; cutting the grass was a pain too. There was a lot of it. But my favorite part of the house throughout my childhood was the basketball court my dad had built for us. Not a full court, but two hoops, pavement, and enough room for me and my brother to treat it like a full court. I'll never forget the first day we went down there. We often played one on one, but when we weren't we were playing two versus nobody. CJ and I versus two imaginary guys that we constantly stole the ball from, fast-breaked on, and threw lob after lob over to one another. I guess this was the first version of Lob City. Safe to say we never lost.

My brother and I enjoyed an excellent childhood at that house, full of love, family, and peace, while still having the kind of mentality needed to always fight and strive for more. We had the perfect mix of comfort and hunger. This allowed us to know the importance of faith and a strong work ethic.

What we did on Saturday nights, though, never mattered because my dad would wake us up at the crack of dawn every Sunday morning. In our family, Sundays were dedicated to church, and my dad didn't play about that.

The only thing that made us feel better about those Sunday mornings were my dad's Eggos. He needs to patent how he makes them or something, Pops was so good at it. While most people just toss them in the toaster, my dad had a way of making them in the oven on broil until they formed into a crunchy, golden, buttery crisp that actually made them look better than the picture on the box. Dad's Eggos were so fire, I feel like I can taste them right now.

Those big breakfasts were extremely needed. We had full days on Sundays. Church didn't start until 11:00 a.m.; however, we had to be up early enough to get ready, eat, and make it to Sunday school, which happened before the actual service.

"Good morning, Dad," CJ would say, digging sleep out of his eyes. "Are you trying to beat the Lord to church?"

"You guys want to ride with me, right?" Dad would reply, laughing, already fully dressed from head to toe before we'd even brushed our teeth. "I'm heading out in about five minutes. Breakfast is ready." It was 8:00 a.m., and the church was twenty minutes away.

"We'll ride with Mom!" CJ and I would both anxiously respond.

My mom would get us there at 9:30 a.m., giving us enough time to enjoy those perfect Eggos and look over our Sunday-school lessons. Now Bible study was on Wednesdays, not to be mixed up with Sunday school. In Sunday school, you had to know your lessons, because you got called on sometimes, and if you didn't know your scriptures or lesson plans, that was a problem.

I still know my Bible. Some of my favorite scriptures are Hebrews 11:1, "Faith is the substance of things hoped for but the evidence of things not seen," and Philippians 4:13, "I can do all things through Christ who strengthens me."

I can quote these Bible verses all day, which is amazing to a lot of people, but not to me. I came up in a Black church in the South, which meant that you were going be there for breakfast, and lunch, and sometimes dinner. Church normally runs about one to two hours; however, a Black church is going to keep you in there singing, praising, listening to the sermon, memorizing those scriptures, watching the congregation worship, and studying the Bible for at least five hours each Sunday. It definitely made for a long day, but it was all that we knew. It wasn't until I went to the NBA and heard about some other services that I realized not every church was like this. Dreamland's hours were from 10:00 to about 5:30, almost every single Sunday. Despite the long hours, Dreamland is home and I'm forever grateful for the foundation it set for me.

Church has always been an amazing way to bring Black people together—no matter where you're from. You can go on any corner in any major city or approach a group of young Black people in the South, and I guarantee you won't find a person that doesn't have stories about their family church. When it comes to church, everything gets much smaller. And this is how community is built, with the Black church being the center. To give a little context to the importance of the church: Christianity is the reason so many captured Black people learned to read, and this education led to freedom.

After the Civil War ended, when America started its long journey piecing itself back together, freed slaves were left with nothing—no land, no opportunity, no pathway to connect with their families who had been stolen and sold, so they turned to their churches. It's important to me that I know this history, mostly so I can pass it on to my kids. It's not something you always get from schools, however, so educating myself and listening to those around me in the Dreamland community was a good way to do that. Now that I'm older, I can truly appreciate what Dreamland Park did for our family.

Papa was a bit younger, but almost the same generation as Martin Luther King Jr., Fred Shuttlesworth, Vernon Jones, and other icons like Bayard Rustin who met when they were planning what we now know as the civil rights movement. The church had been good to Papa and his faith blessed him with so much to be proud of, lessons that he passed down to us. I loved my church and it was always cool to see Papa and my dad, both as deacons—whom I looked at as leaders of the church.

A deacon can be responsible for a lot of things, but when I think about how to define what a deacon does the answer is pretty simple: deacons do what needs to be done. That was their role at the church or at the station: in a nutshell, be the guy who could get things done.

Deacons raise money, they grill at the cookout, help you find money for your business, play shooting guard on the church basketball team, fix your leaky toilet, raise college money for scholarships, put fires out, perform brain surgery, teach the kids karate, all while helping you save money on your taxes. There's nothing that a deacon can't do. That's why it suited Papa so well. I bet if a deacon had an interview where someone asked, "What qualifies you to be a deacon?" they'd have to answer, "Because I have the skills to do anything and everything." The desire to do anything that needs to be done is the only way you'll be able to fill that position.

Dreamland Park is located in the neighborhood of Dreamland, up on a hill, off Martin Luther King Drive over in East Winston, near my great-grandma's house. I think it was Chris Rock who I first heard say something like this, but I find it funny that Dr. Martin Luther King Jr. was one of the most peaceful guys in the history of peace, but most of the neighborhoods that bear his name are not to be played with. You go to any Black neighborhood in any city and there's always a street named Martin Luther King Boulevard, and you already know what time it is.

From afar, our church looks like a huge residence because of the worn siding and brick bottom, but up close, you can see the wide, gray steps that lead to the glass double doors making up the entrance. Across from the entrance stands the blue-and-white Dreamland Park Baptist Church sign, used for advertising upcoming church events and activities—like vacation Bible school, the choir anniversary, the pastor anniversary—or sometimes it just had valuable messages like, "when you are willing, God is able" or "when you run alone it's called a race, when you run with God it's called grace."

The inside of the church is more modern than the exterior. Directly behind the entrance lies a sea of ocean-blue carpet that runs throughout the building—and perfectly matches the same color blue cushion on the upholstered chairs and the blue that surrounds the altar and all the pews, close to where the deacons sat. The overwhelming blue kind of makes you feel like you are relaxing on a stretch of infinite sea. Everything else is oak— oak makes up the frames that support the chairs, the box where members deposit their tithes and offerings, and the pulpit where the pastor delivers his REALLY LONG sermons. As a kid, sitting still and listening to anything that long is damn near impossible. Remember, church was 10:00 to 5:30, but it really didn't feel like we were in there for seven hours, or however long we stayed—because everybody in there was family. Family in a communal sense—the kind of family you can reach out to if you are in a bind, the people you want to call first when you're celebrating a win, or the people strong enough to pick you up after a devastating loss, the people who help you become you.

Regal and strong, Papa would clap and sing along to all the hymns before sitting back and listening to the word delivered by our pastor, all the way up until he would eventually doze off. Now this didn't happen all the time, but you have to remember, Papa was tired after a long week of running his business and being the patriarch of our family. Sometimes he was burned out by Sunday. CJ and I always kept our eyes on Papa during church. I don't know why, but we thought seeing him nod off was the funniest thing in the world. It was the suspense of seeing if he was going to hit his head on the pew behind him. It usually started with a subtle slouch in his chair. If I noticed it first, I'd elbow CJ to make sure he saw, and just doing that was enough to get CJ laughing. At this point, my mom would usually notice and give us that church glare to shut the hell up and pay attention to the pastor. We couldn't help it, though; I'd look over again, and the head nods would start going. Ever so slightly, Papa's head would begin tipping down toward his chest, but he'd wake himself up and shake it off. He'd look around to make sure no one noticed that he'd nodded off and let out two or three "AMENs" like he'd been listening all along, LOL. Once he lost the fight to these nods, his chin would rest on his chest. It was through for him. Truthfully, he'd just look like he was deep in prayer, so most people didn't notice, but once CJ and I saw his glasses start sliding down to the tip of his nose and almost off his face, we'd be laughing so hard, but trying to keep it together. That definitely got us another glare from Mom or Dad. No matter what, though, nobody took offense to Papa catching a few Z's in church because everyone knew how hard he worked and that he needed any rest he could get.

Though I love my church dearly, basketball definitely got me out of some of those long sermons once we were old enough to have our own schedules. CJ and I both played at the YMCA, and the games started at 1:30 on Sundays. So, we'd try to get out of church by 12:30 to get to the Y on time. One of us would say to the other, "Hey, man, tap Mama on the shoulder, 'cause it's time to go. I ain't trying to be late to this game." One of our parents would take us to the game, and if the game was still going on after church let out, then the family and friends from church would show up to cheer us on. It was a pretty special time and moments that I'll always cherish.

7

DON'T QUIT

- -

FIGHTING THE POWER IS GOOD, BUT BECOMING
THE POWER IS EVEN BETTER.

—TOM JOYNER

Tom Joyner was a legendary figure in the Black community throughout the late twentieth century. He was a DJ with his own syndicated show, *The Tom Joyner Morning Show,* which was broadcast throughout the South. If you know, you know, "Ohh, ohh, ohh, it's the Tom Joyner Morning Show!" It was a morning staple of most Black communities. Much more than just a DJ, Tom Joyner was a comedian, a news reporter, and a minister all rolled into one. A huge part of his persona was giving back. Every year, he'd do these big charity givebacks, and one year Papa was fortunate enough to get involved.

For one of these big charity events, Tom picked a gas station in every Black community around the country and gave away gas for one dollar per tank for the whole day. He'd then subsidize the rest with a big donation to the gas station. It was no surprise to us that he picked Jones Chevron to be his stop in Winston-Salem. We were so proud of Papa and couldn't wait for that Saturday to roll around.

Not everyone was excited, though. There was another Black-owned gas station maybe a few miles away, and this guy, when I tell you he was mad he didn't get picked by Tom Joyner, he was HOT. He started telling all his customers and anyone who would listen that Papa mixed his gas with water. His lyin' ass . . . What do you think would happen if you mixed water and gas and then put it into a fuel tank? If you're not a car person, let me educate you: water and gas DO NOT mix. Obviously, this was ridiculous, but the rumor spread. It got back to Papa, and he actually lost customers over it.

Instead of getting hot about it or trying to refute it, he just kept doing his thing. When it came up, he'd just smile, probably take a breath while thinking, *I am blessed and highly favored,* and tell that person the truth. He went through so much just to get his business started that this was just another speed bump along the way. He could have gone crazy or tried to confront that guy, but his confidence led him to not get into it with him.

This caused all kinds of headaches around the Tom Joyner event, because Papa spent more time swatting away that lie than setting up for the actual event. He also spent a ton of time talking my mom and Aunt Rhonda out of going down there and saying who knows what to that guy. They were mad as hell. The day finally came, and it was a family affair. Everyone was there working at the station—cousins, aunts, uncles, friends. It was beautiful. The line was backed up a mile, all the way down to Ackingna's and up past Carver High School. We had to have someone out there directing traffic so the customers could get in and out of the service station.

Papa was beaming that whole day, and I know at least a little bit of that pride was coming from the fact that he knew the man down the road was talking behind his back and he had taken the high road. Those petty rumors didn't keep the cars from coming. Papa got to see his family hustling, and his crew keeping people entertained.

I already mentioned how we work hard in our family. Well, the flip side to working extremely hard is that sometimes things don't work out and you need the mental capacity to be able to deal with that, like when someone gets jealous and spreads lies about you to keep you down. This is part of reaching your full potential personally and professionally. You have to be strong and confident enough in yourself when you don't win. And that means that even if you feel like you worked ten times harder than all your teammates and all your opponents combined. Trust me, it happens. I say this from experience.

Most people don't realize that I didn't even start playing varsity basketball until I was a junior in high school. I played JV in ninth and tenth grade, believe it or not. I believe in my heart I should have been on varsity the moment high school started. This wasn't just because CJ was on varsity, and it wasn't because all the guys on my AAU team already were on varsity. I should have been on varsity because JV was somewhat too easy for me. Night in and night out, I was dropping thirty and ten with a bunch of steals. I lobbied Coach Laton, the varsity coach, over and over to move me up, but he said the same thing every time: "You won't get as much playing time up here, Chris." At this point, my dad and I were like "it's whatever" and agreed I should stay on JV to build my confidence.

Even though I knew I was good enough to be on varsity, the fact that I wasn't didn't mean I was going to hang my head, it just meant I needed to get to work. So, I started practicing with the varsity every day after my JV practice.

We had two gyms at our high school. The old gym, where the JV practiced, had a tile floor. It seemed like the janitor often forgot to clean that court, because the floor was always dirty and slick.

It wasn't anything too bad, but also not an ideal way to improve your game. And then there was the new gym where varsity practiced, which had a fresh wood floor and backboards, and rims that weren't bent out of shape from years of hooping. After school got out, I would go to my JV practice in the old gym. As soon as that practice let out, I'd run over to the new gym to practice with varsity. I did that every single day and never complained about it one bit. At times, I would even go home after both of these practices and still hoop a little bit more. Ball really was and STILL IS life.

All that work seemed to start to pay off when I got moved up to varsity to play an annual Christmas tournament during my freshman year. They didn't let me play the first game or the second. I finally got in the third game, the championship game, but only because CJ had fouled out, but after the tournament, it was right back to JV. Anticlimactic, huh? It felt like the people who coached me on varsity either didn't see it or didn't want to acknowledge it yet. During this period, I talked to Papa all the time.

"Chris," he'd say, "you know how many people

told me I couldn't afford buying my own service station or that my business would fail in the first year because I never ran my own shop before? Did that stop me?"

"No, Papa."

"Keep doing your thing. Trust in yourself, and people will see it. You'll learn from this. I promise."

Both CJ and I wanted to make it to the NBA, and he played varsity all four years, so I thought that I should be able to do the same. After I didn't get to play my first year, I thought for sure I'd be on varsity as a sophomore, but again, it didn't happen. As a young athlete, this was one of the hardest things I ever had to face.

My dad told me that I could have easily made varsity as a sophomore, and my mom wanted me to play with CJ. As much as I wanted to, though, the trade-off was that Coach was still saying I wouldn't get any playing time. That's the part that hurt the most, being denied that chance, because I knew I was good enough. And I still feel the same way, years later: the best player should get the job.

"Chris, it's just politics," my dad would say with a hint of anger. "Don't let these people take you away from your focus. Keep working hard, keep being you." But at this point, I was off Coach Laton.

I believed everything my dad had told me, but it still hurt. Kind words are important, even though they are not enough to erase the feeling of being slighted. Varsity was the show. It didn't really matter to me if I could score a thousand points a game playing JV; no one would notice because they'd all be focused on varsity. I really wanted to be there. I deserved to be there. I thought not being on varsity my first two years of high school was going to affect my career in a negative way, but, looking back, it made me even hungrier. I can now see how it helped me out in more ways than I ever could have imagined at the time.

Every time I get the opportunity to talk to young athletes, I always tell them about my experience on JV, and I tell them that, ironically, it was great for my confidence. Confidence is everything when you step on the court. It's your fuel, the foundation of your trust, and it guides you on how to make decisions. It's everything. *Would I have been able to build the same kind of confidence if I'd been a tenth grader, playing varsity, sitting on the bench?* Probably not.

Not playing on varsity right away gave me the opportunity to really perfect my game. I learned to perfect my ball-handling skills, adjust what I wasn't good at, finish more with my opposite hand, and get used to dominating. It became normal to me to be the one to take over games at that point and I never looked back. By the time I actually made varsity in eleventh grade, everyone already knew I was super nice. Looking back now, starring on JV ended up being one of the best things that happened to me.

When I finally slipped on my varsity jersey at the beginning of my junior year, I easily averaged twenty-five points a game. I went from JV to someone whose name was known across the county. What made me most proud of my ascension is the fact that I didn't quit. Not giving in paid tremendous dividends when I was granted the opportunity to play varsity. From then on, when I was told by anyone that I couldn't do something, I never was disrespectful or made a scene—I just went home and worked even harder.

My talks with Papa over those two years really helped, so I make sure I tell the kids about those days as well; when I wasn't good enough yet, or when I was talented enough and still got overlooked. I would always be looking at the goal beyond what was in front of me. Being the best player on my AAU team wasn't enough, being the best player on my high school team wasn't enough, being highly recruited by college teams wasn't enough. It's always *never enough.*

This all brings me back to Papa's favorite saying: "I'm blessed and highly favored." It's about being grateful we are here—able to compete, and that in and of itself is a blessing. So, if you have that ability, then you should be constantly working extremely hard. In turn, you gain the highest level of confidence. Sometimes, you're the only one who can see your potential, but having that kind of confidence and staying committed to excellence, even when you're the only one that can see it, will strengthen you. Because sometimes, just you and your people knowing is all that matters. You have to keep going, keep trying, and keep fighting and you'll keep getting better and better. One day it will pay off; it did for me, it did for Papa, and it will for anyone that takes these lessons to heart.

8

FATHERS, SONS, AND BROTHERS

When I think about Lil Chris's competitive spirit, I sometimes get more involved because he does not have a big or little brother to push him extra hard. Believe me, being a boy and having a big brother makes a tremendous difference. A huge part of my competitive nature came from having CJ in my life.

CJ is my best friend and my partner in all of our businesses, but we were not always this close.

At this point you can't see one of us without the other, but we went at each other all the time when we were kids. A big part of the friction was that I wanted to be around CJ all the time, and he just saw me as his annoying little brother, always tagging along. If CJ was going to a birthday party, then I wanted to go to that birthday party too. If CJ was going to a sleepover, then I wanted to stay at that sleepover too. And if CJ was going out to hoop, I was damn sure going to grab my sneakers and be right behind him. The moral of the story is that when he thought he was doing something, the reality to me was WE were doing something.

We also fought for any and every reason. We literally wanted to kill each other sometimes.

My kids on the other hand surprisingly love each other and they are close as siblings. They may have their fights here and there, but it's not the same kind of dynamic CJ and I had.

CJ was the older brother, and historically, everyone knows that little brothers always want to do everything in their power to beat their big brothers. It didn't matter what it was; it could have been Monopoly, Jenga, PlayStation video games, or sports. And it is only right that for years, CJ beat me at everything. He was more experienced, craftier, and way stronger. I remember when I was on JV practicing with the varsity, CJ had the power to drop his shoulder and just knock me over on his way to the basket. He'd do the same thing when we played one-on-one out in our backyard. There was literally nothing I could do about it. I didn't have the size and I had yet to start lifting weights, so I couldn't compete with his muscle. Finally, when I picked up a little weight naturally and had my growth spurt, I knew I was ready for him. I was going to go at him every chance I got. It doesn't matter if it's Booray on a plane ride, Connect 4, cornhole or cards I need to win. I always say, "I hate to lose more than I like to win." CJ might find it annoying now when I'm looking over him as he lines up a putt, but he has only himself to blame. He made me this way.

I didn't really start beating CJ consistently until he went away to college. I was a scrawny rising junior when he left, but by the time he came home for Thanksgiving break, I was much stronger. By then, I was dunking everything. He knew that there wasn't much anybody could do about it. I was coming into my own. And I have to credit him—I probably would not have worked on my game so much if I didn't have a brother around always trying to beat me no matter what the competition was. All of us are serious competitors. Even my pops, and especially my mom. She's fierce when it comes to winning and I definitely got that from her. Now CJ would probably not admit this, because he was still the big brother, but I would like to believe that he knew I'd eventually overtake him, ever since the first time he came home from college to visit and I beat him out back.

Even after I beat him that first time, CJ and I would still battle on the court. He was still trying to play bully ball, backing me down, fouling me like crazy. My brother was smart enough to stop playing one-on-one against me at this point. He would do this in the pickup games we played against our friends at the Y. If he wasn't on my team, then I had to prepare for his physicality. But at this point, I had gotten so good, it didn't really matter.

Lil Chris and Cam are hooping now, which is so much fun for me. I love watching them and seeing them train. But the dynamic with me and CJ and the natural resistance an older brother brings can't be replicated.

My parents also played a role in forming my mentality about sports and the kind of competitor I am. This is the main thing I try to work on with my kids. Most parents know that all their children are different and you have to treat them as such. As a father to two very different kids, I know this is true, but there was one incident that gave me a right to be the disgruntled little brother. I also took it as an opportunity to punish CJ on the court again.

CJ was a junior at West Forsyth when I was a freshman. My parents would not let me attend team camp with CJ, who was allowed to go because he was two years older. Team camp is when a bunch of different teams come and stay over at a college or university for a week so they can compete nonstop. This is what high school teams come and do to get ready for their season. It's a time when you're playing around the clock, learning the strengths and weaknesses of each other's games, having fun and building bonds. Team camp isn't always at the same college—it tends to move around—but you get that experience of what it's like to hit the road with your teammates. I never got an explanation from my parents as to why I didn't get to go and CJ did. And as you can see, I'm still mad about it.

Though we were always around each other and in each other's business, we didn't get close as friends until he went away to college. It finally dawned on me when he was packing up and starting to say his goodbyes. Suddenly, I couldn't believe I was losing not just a brother, but a friend. We weren't used to being apart. How was I going to deal with this? When I saw him every day, it was easy for us to be at each other's necks, but now he was going to be four and a half hours away. Who was going to be around to challenge me and make me better?

I'll never forget the day we dropped him off at Hampton University for the first time. I was so happy for him to go off and hoop, but sad about losing him at the same time.

"Are you excited for CJ?" Mom said, turning around to look at me. "We'll be doing this for you in two years!"

"Two college athletes," Pops chimed in.

"Yeah, but why is Hampton so far away?" I replied. I knew it was just in Virginia, but it felt so far.

I was looking out the window, passing signs that said WELCOME TO VIRGINIA, and then a Hampton exit, Hampton River, and then finally the university. CJ's smile stretched from one end of the car to the other as he eyed the acres of land, the beautiful buildings, and his soon-to-be classmates. You could tell he was getting excited about what was ahead.

"I'm going to park right here so we can quickly get CJ's bags up to his room," Pops said, finding a spot close to my brother's new address. I exited the van and reached for one of CJ's suitcases. Besides clothes and sneakers, CJ had a collection of other things that you need when moving into college, like washcloths, towels, a mini fridge, toiletries, a bunch of things like that. We all lugged his things up the steps and into his dorm room. When we were finished, CJ escorted us back to the van and took time to give us all big hugs. I was so happy for CJ, but equally crushed because this goodbye felt so final. I thought we'd never live together again, that I was losing my big brother. Little did I know

that a few years later, we would start my NBA journey living together again.

He closed the door behind me as we loaded back
up in the van, and he waved at us while we pulled
off campus property. I pressed my head against the
window as we drove away, watching CJ disappear
into his new life—and that same Hampton University sign becoming smaller and smaller in the rearview, until the whole campus disappeared.

"You okay back there, Chris?" my dad said, driving toward the exit. "Chris, you good?"

"Yeah, I'm good," I said as I burst into tears, trying to bury my head deep into my T-shirt, trying
not to upset my parents too much, but I couldn't
help it—I had no idea that my brother attending
school would hit me like this.

"Aww, he'll be home every weekend, baby," my
mother said. "It's going to be okay."

"Let it out, son," Dad said. "I know it's tough. We
are going to miss him too."

I dried my tears, thinking about Papa saying
"Get comfortable being uncomfortable," because
CJ being gone was definitely the definition of un-
comfortable, and part of me growing up was learn-

ing to deal with change. CJ was then and still is today a comfort to me in so many ways.

In the beginning, it seemed like everything changed when CJ left. I couldn't get as excited about playing PlayStation anymore. It wasn't the same playing alone, or with anyone else for that matter. I only wanted to try and beat CJ. It's just not the same playing against the computer. I actually stopped playing video games like that once CJ left for Hampton. I was super lonely, but Papa, being Papa, stepped up and filled the void. While CJ was away at Hampton, I hung around the service station even more. I kept completing my small jobs and making my money. Papa and I had become even closer. We hung out after church, would catch basketball and football games, and loved going to our favorite restaurant, Meta's, and getting her famous barbeque ribs and devouring them together while talking about everything. I still missed my brother, but Papa stepped in and made everything okay—that's what best friends are for.

Eventually, my children are going to have to go through the same thing. They are close and intertwined just like CJ and me. In fact, they take it to the next level because CJ and I are so close that Lil Chris and Cam are basically siblings with his kids, my niece and nephew, Carder and Chloe. It's one big, tight-knit family. Sometimes I wonder if Cam will have that kind of reaction when Lil Chris becomes old enough to leave for college, or was it just me.

I felt a different connection to my brother when we packed up the minivan to go see his basketball games—as if now I were the big brother, his protector, or like his coach. I would sit in the front row, eyeing every play, critiquing every move he made inside my head.

I was getting better and better as a ballplayer and learning how to understand the game on different levels, but it wasn't about me and my game; it was about my brother, and I wanted him to be the best. And if I thought he was slighted by his coach or disrespected by another player, I would lose it. Crazy enough, he does the same to me in the NBA now, and it's been that way my whole career. *Though every now and then I have to tell him to sit his ass down!*

I used to be more anxious and nervous during his games than I was at my own. When I was seeing him out there playing and something bad happened, or he missed a shot, I'd be pissed. And sometimes other players would talk crazy to him. At this point, I was really making a name for myself. I wasn't scared of anyone on the court offensively, defensively, mentally, physically—nothing was intimidating me. If anyone was talking crazy to CJ, I'd yell onto the court, "I wish you would say that to me!" But I had to remember, it wasn't about me. I had to learn to relax, fall back, and just cheer for my brother, which I was always happy to do. Except this one time.

It's hard to believe it, but we played against each other in college. CJ had left Hampton and transferred to the University of South Carolina Upstate, or USC Upstate for short. The NCAA changed the rules allowing different colleges from different divisions to match up, and surprisingly, Wake Forest and USC Upstate got a chance to play against each other during a preseason game.

Our whole family showed up to watch us play against each other. My dad even had a hat made— USCU on one side and Wake Forest on the other— because he proudly wanted to support both of his sons. My whole family was covered in USC Upstate, or Wake Forest, or hybrid gear. There are some old photos that I love with what seems like hundreds of my family members snug together at the game wearing T-shirts that said PAUL BALL.

CJ didn't get a lot of playing time in that game, because he got in foul trouble early. He was using his strength to hit other players, the same way he did me for the bulk of my childhood, but this time, the refs were on him. It's crazy because CJ and I only got to match up against each other once. I never got any dunks my freshman year at Wake Forest, but this USC Upstate game was a little different. The energy levels were off the charts, and I actually got my first collegiate dunk of the year during that game. I got a steal, had the open floor, two hands off two feet, and I even thought about hanging on the rim and getting a tech just so I could smile at my brother while doing it. To this day, I regret not doing that, LOL.

The Wake fans went crazy. The game wasn't close at all. It was actually an ass whooping if I'm being honest. We beat the breaks off of them. The final score was 102 to 57. In CJ's defense, our team was stacked full of All-Americans and they didn't really have a shot. But it felt good to play against my big brother, even though it probably didn't feel so good on his end. I even tried to give him a call once I got back on the team bus to make sure he was good, but he didn't want to talk about it. I wasn't trippin' though, because I probably would have been the same way.

Now, twenty years later, it's been so much fun to watch Lil Chris and Cam get into basketball; Cam is warming up to it, Chris loves it more than anything. The kid is a walking basketball encyclopedia. He knows everything about the game, can tell you anything about all his favorite players, both past and present. I always try to bring Lil Chris with me to practice, some games, and especially All-Star Weekend when the game is less intense. You'll never see his eyes wider than when he's meeting the real guys he loves and that he's playing as on NBA *2K*. Even after all these years, he still gets excited, and it means so much to me that we can give that to him and have these experiences with him.

This started at an early age for him, too; one of my favorite moments ever is when I was playing for the Clippers in LA and Blake Griffin and I were doing postgame media. We were asked about a play in the game, and I told Lil Chris, who was in my lap and barely two at the time, to make the "Blake face." Right on cue, right next to one of the biggest stars in the game, Lil Chris scrunched up his brow and put on a mean mug. He made the same face Blake would always make in the game after dunkin' on somebody. You can't teach that. I love that even at that age he had that kind of attention to detail and so much love for the game.

Sometimes I'll even catch Lil Chris in the movie room watching highlights, studying the greats and how they move. Today's kids have such an advantage looking at all the archived footage on YouTube—footage I wouldn't've dreamed of being able to access when I was his age. My hope is that kids won't just watch these moves on their phones but will venture outside to try them out themselves. Me and CJ couldn't wait to try the crossovers and passes we saw our favorite players doing on TV.

As children, me and CJ would always watch the

Bulls whenever we could on WGN, and the next day you could find the two of us outside trying fadeaways, stutter steps, crossovers, up and unders, and gliding with our tongues out just like Mike. CJ and I were Scottie and MJ every chance we got. Me as MJ, and CJ as Scottie—of course slapping the pavement in the backyard, hittin' spin moves at the park, or even when we windmill-dunked rolled-up tube socks into the dirty clothes hamper. That is the kind of energy the game of basketball creates, and I talk about that fire a lot with my kids.

Lil Chris hustles hard on the court and constantly works on his game in a way that makes me proud as he strives to be the best player that he can be. But, there's something special I see when he's in North Carolina, specifically when he's at home, in our gym in Winston-Salem. I think there's something about knowing this was the place that made me into the player I became that just allows him to click into another gear. The Carolina version of Lil Chris reminds me of Papa and me. And I'm not sure if it's because we built our own gym in Winston-Salem or because of the way my Carolina homies Jon Jon and Mike push him, but Chris takes it to a whole different level. He wakes me up at the crack of dawn, saying, "Dad, take me to the gym with you. I'm ready. I want to go early with you."

Taking my name, Lil Chris was born into basketball. He cannot remember a time when the way I performed wasn't a part of a conversation, or living in a house without basketball trophies, basketball awards, and basketball plaques. With my job comes sacrifices we all make as a family. Sometimes it even means taking a rare day off to hop on a flight and fly to see them before we have to be wherever our next game is, or sometimes it's them coming to see me, right when they get out of school. Every moment counts when it comes to family, but time is so much more important when you're living away from home. Basketball has been our lives and we've learned to make the travel part work for us as best we can.

For so much of his life there's been so much focus on basketball, and now at fourteen he's becoming his own person on his own path, trying to figure out what's right for him. For both of my kids, their dreams are of the utmost importance and we will support them in any and all of it.

FATHERS, SONS, AND BROTHERS

As parents, we want to cultivate whatever it is our children want to do. All I ever wanted was for Lil Chris to be passionate about things outside of just video games. Even if that was his main focus, then I'd encourage him to take gaming development classes and become the best at that. I always ask Lil Chris if he loves basketball and promise him that he doesn't have to say what he thinks I want to hear. I would never try to put that kind of pressure on my son, because I want him to be happy, in whatever way he gets there.

"If you say you love anything but remain content knowing that there are people out there working harder than you on their craft, can you really say you love it?" I asked Lil Chris. This is something I'm always saying. Being one of the oldest guys in the NBA, some of my teammates are closer to my son's age than mine. Imagine that. As a vet, some guys try to take shortcuts but I can't do that, it's always been all or nothing.

A while back, one of my coaches in Houston, Brett Gunning, said, "One of the things you're going to have to work on is being able to deal with people that don't care as much as you do." That's one of the best things I ever heard, because I see the sport as more than just a game we play. I care so much because I really, REALLY love basketball and I hate to lose. I think about it all the time, I watch games every chance I get, I study this game daily like a scientist. I am obsessive because basketball is a huge part of my life, and I have a responsibility to my teammates to do what I can to contribute to us winning. That's the kind of love it takes to be successful at the highest level—in basketball or in any other career. These lessons Papa taught me don't just apply to basketball and that's what's so cool about them.

It's been dope to watch Lil Chris develop in basketball over the years but I'll support him no matter what he does. At one point, he was into the other sports so much that he went a year when he didn't play basketball at all. And again, I proudly supported him, I didn't even think about forcing basketball into our conversations at all. I saw that he was really loving soccer, so I started getting into soccer, a sport I never played. All my free time went into learning everything about soccer because Lil Chris was getting really good, and I wanted to be there. Finally, after all the YouTube videos, soccer games, manuals, tutorials, and conversations with other eager soccer parents, right at the magical point where I began to get excited because my son was so excited, Lil Chris got tired of soccer, and he just went back to basketball. But that was a part of his process and an important one at that.

This was around the time I came home because of the pandemic. I was still stuck on the idea that Chris wanted to play basketball and not soccer, so who better to train him than me? It wasn't just about training him, it was about spending time with him. I worked him out the same way my dad would work me out. The way Papa trained me in the shop. Even though I worked at the shop, I was never old enough for my granddad to let me do car inspections, but I wanted to anyway, and I put that energy into rotating tires. There were no kiddie instructions for rotating tires; I had to approach those wheels like a grown man. The same applies for Lil Chris. He had to prepare to be trained in a way that was appropriate for his age, yet I pushed him at the same time.

Cardio, training, and drills, drills, and more drills—everything you can think of, from shooting to passing to dribbling, the combination of every-thing you need to be great. Trying to do my rou-tine was not fun for Lil Chris. I didn't want it to go from me being the reason why he wanted to play basketball to me being the reason why he didn't want to touch a ball at all. I'm not an insane dis-ciplinarian, to be clear. I just wanted to give my son the skills he needed to compete. And many of the things we went over mirrored the same kind of training Dad and Papa used on CJ and me. Dad used to train us like we were preparing for a war, and Papa never let us slack at the service station. This wasn't working for Lil Chris and I was happy one day that he communicated that to me; so, in-stead, we started shifting from me training Lil Chris to doing full family workouts during the early days of the pandemic. That worked much better because we all drove each other to do our best. This was much more productive for us than just Lil Chris and me on the court hooping.

When CJ and I were small kids, we always wanted to go with our dad to watch him play basketball. Even though he played football in high school,

Dad loved basketball and would be on teams and leagues throughout Winston-Salem. We would be all over the place, running on the worn wooden bleachers, just watching my dad hoop. Rooting for my dad really helped us develop an early love for the game—we wanted in. The love of basketball was a gift from my father that I've always wanted to pay forward. CJ and I told Dad how bad we wanted to play, and he responded like a dad who loves his kids and knew how much we loved the game.

When we were four and two, Dad bought two of those little plastic Fisher Price Nerf Goals and constructed a full court in our basement. He used red electrical tape to create makeshift foul lines, and we went to work, running back and forth from line to line just like the pros. When we grew a little older, Dad built a basketball court at the bottom of the hill behind our home, so that CJ, the neighborhood kids, and I could hoop anytime we wanted to. Once Dad saw us taking extra interest in the game of basketball, that's when the real training started.

My brother and I were the hardest working five- and seven-year-olds you ever saw in your life. My dad was also a fan of the NBA. He loved how good George "the Iceman" Gervin was with his left hand as a right-handed player, so he wanted that for CJ and me. Dad used to tie our right hands behind our backs so we could do anything with our left. And on the basketball court, he used to make us tuck our right arms inside of our T-shirts so that we couldn't even use that hand at all. And once our left hands developed and we could finish with both, Dad started blindfolding us on the court so we weren't able to just follow the ball with our eyes. It was confusing at first, because CJ and I would run into each other, or into the basket, but we figured it out. One of the proudest moments I had in the NBA was when I was able to introduce my Dad to the Iceman himself at the NBA Legends brunch. As I knew he would, the first thing Daddy told him was how he tied our hands behind our backs so we could learn to play like he played. George enjoyed that, but if only he knew how unenjoyable that discipline was to us at the time.

Given all this training he was doing, one thing that my daddy hated more than anything was lowering the hoops. He did not play that at all. He was training us like adults and thought this would instill bad habits in our games. Every kid wants to lower the rim to throw lobs and dunk like they're Dominique Wilkins. We were kids at the time, so you know CJ and I lowered the goals while Daddy was at work. Now remember, there were no iPhones, no digital alarm clocks, so we didn't know when he would be pulling up. Those days he caught us in the driveway dunking sideways and backward and throwing alley-oops. Pops would get out of his car yelling, "Put those goals back up!"

He was mad because he was training us to be better, but also because we had broken the first two rims by hanging on them, doing our best Darryl Dawkins impressions. I laugh now thinking about the first time I saw Lil Chris dunk on somebody after lowering the rim, remembering how my dad didn't play that. When it came to Lil Chris, I saw what my dad was thinking. The last thing a father or grandfather wants to do is make things too easy for their kids. They need resistance to get better—it goes back to Papa teaching us to be relentless—but damn, it was fun to dunk like a seven-footer when the rims were lowered by two feet. Those big guys have it easy as hell.

Once those rims went back up, it was right back to Dad's strict methods, which meant no horsing around. Dad's methods worked so well that by the time CJ began playing AAU, he felt very comfortable dribbling with his left hand as a right-handed person—and I experienced the same. Once I got to high school, I was way ahead of the game because my father already had me thinking and training like a pro.

Dad wanted CJ and me to be the best, so he trained us to be the best, and I can honestly say I hated it all the way up until I loved it. Even now, I get up extra early so I can get to the gym early because I love it. It's fun to me. I am very open when my strength and conditioning team has new things to try. You always have to be willing to continue to get better. My trainers Donnie and David are always pushing me to new levels and I love it.

As such, my training, diet, and game have evolved, but the one thing that hasn't changed is my work ethic. I still train as hard as I used to, nothing has changed in that regard. The team around me embraces a work-smarter mindset to make sure every little thing I'm doing achieves the bigger goal. Communication means that all systems are working together and I'm doing everything I can to keep my body and mind ready for top performance. I'm beyond lucky to have the best of the best around me.

It wasn't just about working hard on the court for my dad; we saw him work extra hard at his jobs, just so CJ and I could play basketball. We try and help our kids understand how the sacrifices their grandparents and great-grandparents made created the life that they enjoy. In the same way, CJ and I as kids didn't see that some of Papa's choices would send us in in the right direction.

This probably all sounds like a lot of intense, tough love, but I truly believe that I have the best parents in the world. And that's why I'm so hard on my kids. Every dollar, every minute, and every piece of energy my parents had went into CJ and me when we really got into basketball. It felt like my parents gave so much of themselves in order to focus on our basketball dreams. This was before we even had careers, before people said we were gifted. My dad only got one paid week off per year, so he would have to take out a loan or put in extra hours at Papa's shop just to have enough money to pay the bills. Dad always had to take off for at least two or more weeks so that he could come to all our AAU games. Our teams were always good. We made it to the Nationals every single year, so we needed him to be there, coaching us, looking out for us, and making sure we were doing our best. Dad never complained or made excuses, he just made it happen. And my mom also came to every game we played, always cheering us on. Having one parent, let alone both, as well as an extended family, attending so many basketball games is such a blessing. I am forever grateful because I know so many people don't have that luxury.

I always laugh at the way my mom couldn't stand being at my games when the score was close. She might say it was time for her to go to the bathroom or she just needed a break. But I knew it was the unbearable anxiety of seeing if I was going to close the game out or not. I even remember being on the free throw line a few times during some of those close games, and I could clearly see her making her way through the crowd, saying, "Excuse me, excuse me," stepping past and over people, trying to get out of the gym. Some of the other moms or my classmates would run to the bathroom to give her updates, like, "Chris just hit a three—it's over! We won! You can come out!" Relieved, she would walk out of the bathroom and sneak back to her place in the stands like she'd never left. I love the way my parents love me, and they continue to show me that love over and over again, even to this day.

As our basketball journeys advanced, my dad ended up spending his entire 401(k) on AAU. Obviously, we didn't know how brave a decision that was back when we were little kids, but now I understand what that means. And I'm even more grateful, because so many people never have a person to believe in them like that, and I'm proud that my parents' huge sacrifice didn't go to waste. As a matter of fact, one of my proudest days is when I told my dad that he could walk into work and tell his boss that his days on the assembly line were over and that he was going to retire. He was proud of his work, but I would be able to take care of him the same way he'd taken care of us.

In these moments, I begin to evaluate myself and reflect on the decisions I've made. On the surface, I honestly always just work my hardest: I leave it all on the court after every game, I work hard to provide my family security, but people question what makes me keep going, especially at age thirty-eight. It's hard because in theory it would be easier to stop at this age, but I have so much more to accomplish and so much more to give. I'm counting my blessings that I still have the ability to play at the highest level and a love for the game that drives me every day. I'm constantly trying to balance things between family and basketball. I want to be as present as possible in my kids' lives, but it's something I think every working parent wrestles with no matter what you do for a living. A true work-life balance is unrealistic, but you have to just try and be the best version of yourself in both lanes.

Papa would always say, "Time is the one thing

you can't buy, but you have to spend every single day." Am I doing the right things with my time? I often ask myself. I think about Papa, and how his time was cut short by his business and his commitment to our family and the community. I also think about my dad and how he was always present, spending time with CJ and me while working as hard as he could.

Even though my dad worked Monday through Friday, and many, many Saturdays, he still made time to coach us in all kinds of leagues—football, basketball, and everything else we played—while keeping us fit with his rigorous training schedule. The only time my dad didn't coach us was when my mom coached my team at the YMCA, way back when I was in the eighth grade.

Even though my mom is super sweet, she can get real feisty. My mom got a tech the very first game of the season before learning to keep her cool on the sideline. Come to think of it, maybe that's where I get it from. . . .

We were called the No Limit Soldiers, and Mom coached us to a championship. That means at least one of my parents coached every team I ever played on from youth leagues all the way up until I was headed to college. I'm so blessed for that and appreciate how they went from coaching me to being my biggest fans in the stands.

9

THE GAME

Parkland High School, Winston-Salem
Parkland vs. West Forsyth High
November 20, 2002

At this point, I had never seen so many people at a Parkland game. I mean, they were a solid team, but not the kind of school that drew standing-room-only crowds.

Our local basketball scene was changing, and the hype around me as a future college player had everybody in the building. It was also not lost on me that people saw the news all week about my family and wanted to see what tonight's game would bring. It's sad to say, but maybe they wanted to see how I would handle this incredibly difficult situation. Either way, it was loud as hell in there but almost completely silent in my head. Most of my family was there and made up the visitors section. Seeing them was the comfort I needed to push through.

"Keep going, bro. Stay strong!" a teammate said.

I nodded my head in acknowledgment, but didn't say too much, because I didn't want any extra attention on me. For anyone who knows me—truly knows me—they know that I only care about winning. Winning always comes first, so I wasn't trying to put on any kind of a spectacular show. Yes, I remember what Aunt Rhonda had said about honoring Papa, but anything I did, special or not, had to come naturally in the flow of the game—it would never consist of me forcing anything for my own, selfish goal of creating a moment. I honestly don't know how to play any other way but to try to win the game.

"How you feel?" DG asked.

"I'm good."

"Let me know what you need," he answered.

DG was genuine. He knew how close I was to Papa, and he had kept talking to me the whole game, not to pry, but to offer real support. Sometimes it wouldn't even be about words. During time-outs, he might put his arm around me, pulling me in. He was my guy, and he wanted to be there for me, even without having to say anything. When really bad things happen, I tend to get extremely quiet—I think the silence helps me to collect my thoughts and craft a way forward. When we see people suffering, sometimes our first instinct is to talk their heads off with words of sympathy. But early on I learned that it's not about saying words, but really asking to see what you can do and reading the room for how you can help. If someone asks for a favor, do it, and if they say, "Nothing," then it is perfectly okay to give them space and just leave them alone. I was in that *leave me alone* stage.

I quietly sat in the locker room, looking into space. Coach Laton was doing what coaches do, pacing back and forth, discussing strategy—what to look out for during the second half. I tried to listen, but, as you can imagine, I wasn't focused on Coach at that moment. I was too consumed by my thoughts, trying to compartmentalize everything that was going on and how I could get through this game.

I know there was a halftime, but I don't remember it. I'm sure the team was hype because we were winning, but I was just all in my head, thinking uncontrollably. I remained silent, because all I could think about was Papa—and how he would be mad at me, standing over me fussing, talking about, "Why'd you wait so long to put on a show like this, Chris? You could have been doing this all along. Now keep going!"

Imagining Papa in the building made me smile. Knowing he wasn't there then started to overwhelm me, but I couldn't let the emotions take over. I needed to get through this game and get a win.

THE GAME

"Chris, you ready?" Coach Laton said as I blankly stared at a locker.

"Yes sir, on my way," I said, snapping out of my daze and making my way back toward the court.

10

DON'T CHEAT THE DEACS

- - - - - - - - - - - - - - - - - - - -

THE ABCS OF LIFE GO LIKE THIS:
A STANDS FOR ACADEMICS,
THE B STANDS FOR BASKETBALL, AND
THE C STANDS FOR CHARACTER.
—COACH SKIP PROSSER

The three most influential men in my life have been Papa, my dad, and my college coach, Skip Prosser.

I knew Coach Prosser was a special guy the first time I met him in Orlando, Florida, at an AAU tournament. I was in high school, trying to impress college coaches and scouts. Colleges from all over the country sent me letters, came to check out my games, and worked extremely hard to recruit me. Growing up in North Carolina, I was a die-hard Tar Heel fan. Despite all the attention I was getting, that's where my heart still was at the time. Michael Jordan had every kid from North Carolina—and every future hooper for that matter—dreaming of running up and down the court in that Carolina Blue.

I was the biggest Tar Heel fan and could name every player from guys like Dante Calabria, Donald Phelps, Derrick Phelps, Donald Williams, and Ed Cota, to Sam Perkins, James Worthy, and, of course, the best to ever play the game, Michael Jordan. I attended the Carolina Basketball camp as a kid, where you train like crazy, and the highlight was that I even got to take a photo next to the legendary coach Dean Smith.

I would do anything and everything to be connected to UNC. CJ and I had a cousin named Shandra, and she and her sister Sherri used to babysit us. Shandra dated superstar UNC wingman and former NBA All-Star Jerry Stackhouse. We used to get dropped off at her house regularly, but this one particular day I remember like it was yesterday. CJ and I were in the kitchen, minding our business and eating our bowls of cereal, and then Jerry Stackhouse walked in. Thinking about seeing such a legend and then actually seeing him were two entirely different things, and it blew my mind. My brother and I tried really hard to keep our cool and not act like fans, but we were and couldn't help ourselves. Before we knew it, he was asking us about basketball, whom we played for, and even took us out back to hoop in the driveway. Years later, after Stack was drafted by the Philadelphia 76ers, he sent my whole AAU team Filas. That made me love Carolina even more. It was my dream to attend UNC, but meeting Coach Prosser and seeing his vision changed everything.

I first became aware of Coach Prosser the summer before my junior year in high school. I remember being in Florida during AAU Nationals. It was the same way back then as it is today, except now you just can see more highlights on YouTube and can livestream the games. At tournaments like that, you see coaches from every part of the country, the best coaches from some of the biggest programs, checking out games and seeing who is doing what. Coach Prosser was in a group of coaches checking out the games. There was no grand introduction between us because you were only allowed to talk to coaches during open periods per the NCAA regulations, but I knew who he was. I just walked past him, and said, "Hey, what's up, Coach?" and kept moving.

George Edward "Skip" Prosser grew up in Carnegie, a suburb right outside of Pittsburgh. He played basketball at the United States Merchant Marine Academy, where he studied nautical science. Coach P was a lover of biographies, history, and philosophy. His favorite quote was from the essayist and philosopher Ralph Waldo Emerson, which read, "Our chief want is someone who will inspire us to be what we know we could be." And that's exactly what Coach spent his career doing.

Coach got his big break when he was hired by Xavier University as an assistant to Pete Gillen. He spent a few years there until landing the head coaching job at Loyola University in Baltimore. But Coach only stayed there for one year, because Gillen left Xavier, and that head coaching job had his name all over it. Coach took the job and became the second-winningest coach in the school's history at the time before making his way to Wake Forest.

As time progressed, I would see Coach Prosser here and there at basketball games, and I got real excited when he actually made his way to see me. When you're young, you notice coaches at your game. It's a great feeling to know that people on the next level have an interest in seeing you play. There are scouts, assistant coaches, and other people on the team at games all the time, but when you see the head coach pull up, you know it's serious.

What I loved about Coach Prosser from the beginning was that he wasn't flashy. When he came in, he didn't always sit front and center like the other coaches. He might sit over to the side solo, laid-back, holding his little notebook, taking notes. Coach would simply watch whom he came to watch and then quickly get out of there without trying to make himself known. He was about his business. Even when I got to high school and he started coming to my games, he maintained the same calm and cool demeanor. I could be coming off a game where I had just put on a show and he wouldn't appear to be impressed at all.

After the game, he might just pull me to the side and say something like, "Are you ever going to play some defense?" He didn't follow it up with a laugh, because it wasn't a joke. Coach would be dead serious, pausing only to reiterate, "Play some defense, Chris." It's even more special now that I'm looking back at it, because he was pushing me to do better than other high school basketball players right off the bat. Defense becomes more of a focus in college and he wanted me to be ready. His influence pushed me to be militant about playing defense even now at the NBA level. I really believe defense is indicative of your work ethic; if you're working harder than the other guy, you're going to be successful at it. I tell that to my teammates, my AAU teams, my kids, anyone who wants to be great and take their game to the next level. I appreciate you, Coach, for that.

Maybe Coach was trying to get me ready for

college, but at the time, I still had that high school attitude all kids develop. You know the one: "You can't tell me nothing! I ain't tryna hear it!" Especially because I was starting to become a real problem on the basketball court.

At the same AAU Nationals where I met Coach Prosser for the first time, we played against the star-studded Illinois Warriors seventeen-and-under team, who had Andre Iguodala, Shannon Brown, and Dee Brown on their squad. These were three of the best players in the country at the time. My team was only sixteen and under so some of those guys were a full year older than us. A year matters big-time at that age and level.

With all that talent on the court at one time, our game was the main event for all the coaches in attendance. The Warriors were supposed to win it all and easily beat our younger team from North Carolina. All the coaches wanted to recruit the Warriors' rising senior stars to their colleges. They came for the Warriors, but stayed to see our team, Kappa Magic. We surprised people with our fight and I loved it. Unfortunately, we lost the game, which still bugs me to this day. Even though they

were older, we almost pulled it out as major under-
dogs. We only lost by five points. Scoring thirty-six
points in that game was the start of all the national
attention I received from then on out.

I began receiving stacks and stacks of mail, and
it became a daily event. Coach Laton was also my
history teacher, and I had him for seventh period,
the last period of the day. So every day, I'd stroll
into class, and a huge pile of letters from different universities was waiting for me. Everybody in
my class would be like, "Dang, Chris, look how
many came today. Look how many came today,
Chris." There were so many schools writing to me,
even colleges that I'd never heard of. I was smart
enough to know which letters were just a filled-in
template, "Dear Chris, blah, blah, blah, blah,
blah." That kind of interest didn't feel genuine. I
could tell they had sent that same letter to a ton of
other guys. The one place I wasn't hearing from,
though, was UNC. I didn't know what more I had
to do. Schools from all over the country were hearing about me and sending me letters. It killed me
that the one school I was obsessed with, in my own

home state, couldn't spare a stamp to send me a generic interest letter. My frame of mind started to change at that point. Part of me wanted to just turn my back on UNC, but an even bigger part of me still really wanted that letter.

I remember my UConn letter specifically because that school was so far away from home to me. And I opened it thinking, *How do they even know about me?* But I later found out Coach Jim Calhoun from UConn was at that same game against the Illinois Warriors. Coach Calhoun and Tom Izzo from Michigan State both started recruiting me really hard after that. Their sentiment was similar: *We've seen you play this one game, and we want you to come. We want you to come here.*

The interest kept picking up, and it really started to become overwhelming. I could eliminate the generic letters easily because of their lack of effort. Then there were more creative attempts that stuck out. Buzz Peterson, the coach at Tennessee at the time, had a picture of him and Michael Jordan in his letter. Instead of writing a long letter, he'd put a little speech bubble coming out the side of Michael Jordan's mouth that read, "Hey, Buzz, you really need to go get that kid, Chris Paul!" The job for coaches when sending these letters was to be memorable and that sure worked.

I say all of this about the other letters to say that my letter from Wake Forest was one of a kind. It was folded, and on the outside, it read. "Wake Forest Basketball." Then when I opened it, the smooth paper didn't have any lines on it. It was just plain white. But the sentences that were written were so straight they gave off the feel that there were invisible lines that the writer had used. Later on, I found out they used to put a ruler on the paper and write the letter to you, slowly and carefully, line by line, in the neatest penmanship you've ever seen in your life. The attention to detail here was so incredible. The craftsmanship and beauty of those letters made me feel special, like I was somebody important, and that I was being welcomed to a school that was going to treat me that way.

What I also appreciated was how Coach Prosser actually recruited me himself. I appreciate people like Doug Wojcik, who was an assistant coach at Carolina at the time, Chris Collins, who was an assistant coach at Duke at the time, and all the other assistant coaches who were recruiting me too. It just felt different, though, having the head coach show interest in you. It's kind of like going in for a job interview, and instead of meeting with a bunch of partners, you get to talk to the CEO, the person in charge, the one who calls all the shots.

In sports and business, it's always a major statement if you're talking to the direct decision maker—along with her or his team. That's why today I am so involved with a lot of my business partners myself. There are some conversations that you should have directly.

While Coach Prosser was recruiting me to be a Demon Deacon, I was also hearing from another Carolina school, NC State. NC State was more accessible than Wake Forest. For starters, Wake Forest is a private school that sits on a campus surrounded by beautiful trees. It was always a little mysterious to me even though it was right in my backyard. You can't just pull up and stroll around at Wake Forest, or you will be stopped by the guards at the gate. The student population at Wake Forest was also small, around four thousand at that time, and the

Black students on campus tended to be athletes for the most part. These are all things I had to consider before choosing that school. And then there was basketball.

NC State told me if I came to play there, they'd give me the ball on my first day and I wouldn't even have to compete for the starting position. Starting wasn't a given anywhere else. I liked the idea of potentially being able to change the tempo of their game. I was more of an up-tempo player and I liked to run, while they played more of a Princeton style offense.

I had also started hanging around some of Wake Forest's games and meeting some of the players like Justin Gray and Josh Howard—who was from my hometown. I had a great relationship with J Gray, because we were close in age and he played my position. Seeing him star at Wake Forest was truly inspiring. The Demon Deacon fans almost had me ready to commit to the school before my official visit, especially after seeing the gym erupt during those games. The noise was like nothing I'd ever heard before, but the second I did, I loved it. Wake Forest had started feeling like home.

Back then, a prospective player was allowed to take up to four official visits to prospective schools, but I only needed one. Official visits are the only time when schools can pay to have you visit their campus. Schools would entertain you (kinda like in *He Got Game*, LOL), feed you a great meal at a nice restaurant, and show you everything they have to offer, all in an effort to get you to pick them. The official visit I took to Wake Forest was scheduled to last from Friday to Sunday and began at the Marriott in downtown Winston-Salem, where we stayed over the weekend. Even after a career in the NBA and all the nice hotels we stay in, I vividly recall that Marriott Hotel. It seemed like a palace to me at the time. I had never been in a hotel that big and flashy before. It seemed like a place where only kings and queens would stay.

Upon entering the hotel and making my way across what seemed like never-ending fancy floors, I was greeted by Coach Prosser and some of his assistants who had also helped recruit me. The group was all smiles as they took me up to my room. The suite was decked out in Wake Forest gear. There was even a beautiful cookie cake decorated with

CP3 in big letters. I had never seen anything like it. From there, they took me to dinner at a restaurant named Village Tavern, which is one of the fanciest spots in Winston-Salem. My family had never eaten there before. The waitress was prepared for my visit; she already knew my name and offered me a custom menu that had all kinds of CP3-themed items for us to eat like the CP3 Pot Stickers and a bunch of other personalized and basketball-themed dishes. I couldn't believe they were doing all this for me—really—all this for me. The moment hit me then that I was being recruited to play basketball at a top university, and I wasn't asking them for the opportunity. It was the opposite. They rolled out the red carpet to convince me, young Chris Paul from Winston-Salem, on the other side of town, to go hoop there. That meant the world to me and it still does.

The next part of my visit took place on campus. A group of players brought me down to the men's locker room, where there was a big picture of me on one of the lockers, with a nameplate that said: PAUL #3. After that, we got a chance to walk over to the Coliseum, where I played some of my high school games, and where Wake Forest played home games. It was pitch-black on the court, until someone hit a switch and I saw a jersey light up in the rafters, again: PAUL #3. I imagined myself wearing that jersey, being on the court, with my whole family in the stands watching me get to play college ball—the thought gave me goosebumps. They really pulled out all the stops, making me feel like a star.

Sunday quickly arrived, and we were set to spend the last day of our visit at Coach Prosser's house. This is when I really began to feel like I got to know Coach. I knew he was a genuine person and someone that I could learn so much from. I thought he was going to do a bunch of talking and show me old pictures or tell me his life story, but we actually had so much more of a back-and-forth conversation. He was asking me questions and talking about how Wake could raise my game to the next level. After that conversation, Coach Prosser did something I really respected. He got super direct with me and just asked, "Okay, Chris, are you ready to commit?" That's Coach, he's not going to waste any unnecessary time.

I was taken aback at first, but in thinking about it now, I respect it. My initial reaction was to hesitate. "Whoa, Coach, are you guys even going to let me think about it?"

Later on, I found out that this was part of the system in place. Colleges that really want you try to get you to commit instantly, especially if your first official visit is with them. They do it because they want to try to hold you to the honor system just in case they are outdone by another school. If a prospective student takes some more visits, coaches want your commitment to them to be the last thing on your mind. My visit to and offer from Wake Forest took place on May 3, 4, and 5 and then the next day, May 6, just so happened to be my seventeenth birthday. And then that elusive call from UNC finally came in. So NOW they wanted me . . . and I finally was offered that scholarship I always wanted. FINALLY! Little did they know, it was too late, and I was already in love with Wake Forest. It really is crazy to think that the opportunity to play for the Tar Heels finally came—the team I'd grown up idolizing.

During the whole recruiting process, I knew that

Raymond Felton was going to North Carolina. Ray was super nice, a year older than me, but the same position, coming out of South Carolina. Crazy how life happens, he actually ended up being my teammate when I played for the Clippers—one of my favorite teammates of my career. Matt Doherty, who was their head coach at the time, told us that I could walk on at Carolina and maybe get a scholarship once Ray went to the NBA. I was *not* trying to hear that. At the time, Doherty didn't even seem that interested. Fast-forward a year later, on my birthday, he was offering me a scholarship. At that point, I had exactly what I wanted. UNC finally offered me a scholarship. It truly satisfied me to know that I could have gone to UNC if I'd wanted to. Once the dream of getting an offer from UNC was realized, I decided to make it official with Wake.

Placing my pen to sign the letter of intent to go to Wake was one of the best decisions I ever made in my life, and I made that decision because of Coach Prosser.

After I committed to Wake Forest, I would go over and watch the guys practice to see how hard Coach was and how he interacted with them. I loved the way he held them accountable, the work ethic he preached, and no matter how popular a player was, he never let them cheat the work. He'd always say, "Don't cheat the Deacs!"

Coach P was all about putting work in, just like Dad, just like Papa. I have now come to appreciate the preseason conditioning, which was so hard that avoiding it was one of the reasons I went to the league. That type of conditioning is CRAZY. He'd make us run a mile in six and a half minutes, at 6:00 a.m., in the freezing cold. Coach didn't send assistants to complete this task either. He was out there himself, shivering from cold with a cup of hot chocolate, watching us work.

I wanted to be a part of that. Coach built a community at Wake Forest, and I knew from Papa how important community was to uphold your values and achieve your goals. It's crazy to think about, even at that age, how much I enjoyed the grind. Again, that's a big thanks to Papa.

11

COMMUNITY

BLOOD MAKES YOU RELATED, BUT
LOYALTY MAKES YOU FAMILY.
—AUTHOR UNKNOWN

It was little things that showed me how special and close my family always was. Every *single* morning, my mom, Aunt Rhonda, and Papa were on the phone. My brother, CJ, and I would be fighting in our room or playing out back before school and I'd hear my mom on the white cordless phone.

She'd be on with them while making us breakfast, talking about this and that, who's doing what, or what basketball or football game she had to go to that night. As close as I am to my own parents and my brother, there's no way we'd be setting up conference calls every morning just to chitchat. Eventually, Papa had to go to the service station, and we'd be right behind him, hopping in Mom's car to take the twenty-minute drive across town to meet him there.

Mama did any and everything with that phone up to her ear, laughing as the three of them would go on and on.

"Tell Papa and Aunt Rhonda we said hey!" CJ and I would interrupt as we greeted Mom and grabbed our food.

I imagine Papa on the other end of the phone, adjusting his glasses and taking a puff of his cigarette while he talked to his baby girls. Papa was responsible for waking up my house, every single day. Sometimes he would be at home, and sometimes he'd be in the car with his bookbag-sized car cellular phone. It's hard to imagine now, especially for my kids, but we didn't have smartphones back in the day. We had super-heavy mobile phones that you had to plug in to your cigarette lighter and carry around in the bag because they wouldn't fit in anyone's pockets. And to make matters worse, the only color they came in was tan. And what's even crazier is that only the coolest people had them, and Papa was definitely one of them.

Papa always put family first. He didn't have to say it, he just showed that we mattered through his actions. I'm so proud to be a product of that. Simply saying that you're doing something is not as valuable as actually doing it. Papa specialized in actions that went far beyond just doing the work, but also taught his family the work. We are nothing without family and community. This isn't just about transactional relationships. It's about asking yourself what are you doing to pour into those relationships, and that place, with the intention of making it better than it was before you got there? Papa exhibited that type of commitment to community in a way that was contagious, and I'm glad that I caught it. You can tell someone something or you can show them. I think it's important to do both, and I know Papa did too. Instead of just saying,

"We should be doing this or that," he went out there and did it. That leading by example struck me then, and it's something I've tried to emulate every day since.

By now, I'm sure it's clear that to know me is to know my family.

If you've ever seen the movie *Soul Food,* you know what I'm talking about—it's not perfect, but it's full of love and joy. The story revolves around a strong matriarch named Mother Joe, Big Mama, who is the heart and soul of her family. When drama arises, you can always count on Big Mama to solve the problem over a hefty plate of food, equipped with greens, macaroni and cheese, fried fish, fried chicken, fried okra, yams, and some kind of cake. Suddenly, Big Mama is hospitalized and she slips into a coma and passes away, leaving her kids and grandkids to deal with their issues on their own. Initially, they struggle, but ultimately they are able to move on as she planted all the right seeds in them.

That was us. I talk a lot about the plant-based

diet I've adopted over the last few years, so it's even a little hard for me to stomach how we used to eat like that. The word "soul" is important here, because even though my diet has changed, my soul hasn't.

The way that movie showcases how connected families can be was like watching my own family on-screen the first time I saw it. I just showed it to my kids recently, and they said the same thing. They both loved the movie and I'm so glad that Jada and I got to watch it with them.

Early in career, when I'd come home every summer, my family and I would have big *Soul Food*–like family dinners every Thursday. This was my way, after a long season, of getting that time with my family. The gathering and fellowship of family would always have everyone eating up all the fish, mac and cheese, salmon croquettes, pinto beans, tuna, potato salad, and everything else the family cooked—while the whole family on both sides was chopping it up and just having the best time. Not much has changed, really. We prioritize family dinners all the time. My whole family isn't fully plant-based, but we prioritize our health overall and that makes me happy. The amount of seaweed chips my kids consume now rivals any amount of fried chicken we used to devour.

Another *Soul Food* theme was church and the community around it. The family around you is built inside that building but extends and connects to everything in your life outside of it. I wouldn't be here if it weren't for Dreamland. Literally. My whole family structure and social life were centered around our church community. My friends, my brothers' friends, and their friends all came from church, school, or sports.

It's the culture around the Black church that is not talked about enough. Papa taught me to never be afraid of who you are and what you believe. This translated into how I saw basketball. I live that today and go back to that during hard moments in my life. When I got traded to Oklahoma City and all of the NBA media counted me out, I just centered myself and focused on my work.

When I think about those early church teachings, I still live by values that are important for family and faith. Am I perfect? Hell no, not even close. I very much learned the importance of the people who mold you and how you can give back to the people who gave to you. Papa put so much of his time, energy, and money into the church, and in turn, he never lacked for customers; they were always there for him. Community is a two-way street, and you have to give and get to really make the most of it.

12

SOCIAL RESPONSIBILITY

IF YOU WANT TO GO FAST, GO ALONE,
BUT IF YOU WANT TO GO FAR, GO TOGETHER.

—AFRICAN PROVERB

That single quote captures the strongest part of my belief system. I am blessed that this was another lesson Papa instilled in me back when I was so young that I probably didn't even understand I was receiving it and would end up carrying it with me for the rest of my life. Papa made good money at the service station. It's no secret. His success was extremely impressive, but his legacy isn't about his finances. Because whatever money Papa made was less important than the way he chose to treat people.

Sometimes I get mad when elders look down on young people as if they never made mistakes and always had everything figured out. More so though, I get mad when the kids won't listen to those who have experience who came before them. Papa didn't pick or choose young or old; he literally treated everyone the same way. If you made some mistakes or were misunderstood, Papa didn't judge you or turn his back on you. In fact, he'd pull you closer, pray for you, and help you in any way he could. He knew it would take his whole community further as a result. He did this for so many people, and not just family members, but also guys in and around the station, the formerly incarcerated, and anyone who was struggling to find their footing. The story of George Durham comes to mind.

George was a cool younger guy from Winston, but

at that point he was going through a rough patch. By the time he was a teenager, he'd developed a pretty bad reputation and was known for being a trouble-maker. He didn't listen to anyone and he was challenging to deal with. Even though all those things were true, anyone who came to know George knew he had a good heart. His missteps were harmless, misinformed, victimless, and came from a place of deep trauma that he wasn't able to get over on his own. Today, we know that he had developmental challenges and deserved a different type of attention from his teachers. Sadly though, back in those days, acting out was strictly attributed to behavioral problems. People like George were considered "bad kids," "lost causes," whatever you want to call them, and then the system would leave them to fend for themselves. After George had a few run-ins with the law, word got back to Papa. This was actually a rule of thumb. Word always got back to Papa! He reacted the way we knew he would, by giving George a job at the service station. George was not going to be written off on his watch. George needed a structure and a skill, and Papa was great at delivering both.

A lot of people thought that Papa was overextending himself by hiring someone who didn't know the difference between a gas cap and a hubcap, but Papa always looked beyond what everyone else saw. He focused on how to bring out the good in everyone and how to provide for others when you are able. Be the change you want to see. Papa did this effortlessly.

George's issues could have come from a number of problems; beyond the fact that he was denied a proper education, he also grew up without a father in a community that lacked resources. Papa knew all about his background when he swooped in and started treating George like a son. And, of course, if Papa treated you like family, then by default, you were our family too. Once George committed to working for Papa, my dad stepped in and made sure he had a ride to and from work every day.

Papa gave George a blue uniform and taught him anything and everything about cars and working at a service station. George became an expert, learning everything from how to perform oil changes and changing brakes to replacing air filters and picking up cars and putting them in the wrecker. He was able to master all those skills without one moment of any formal training to be a mechanic, like most of the full-time people who worked at Papa's shop. Under Papa's guidance, George went from being someone who was written off to a hard worker with plenty of marketable skills. My family had a front-row seat to this transformation, watching Papa mold George into someone who could really contribute and earn in real time. The beauty of it all is that Papa didn't do it for charity purposes—he did it because it was right. It was the kind of social responsibility that has stuck with me and that we all try and bring to my family's foundation, the Chris Paul Family Foundation. We think about what he did for George, or how he provided a safe space for Happy. Papa was just an everyday hero, employing people when they couldn't find work. Once they got on their feet, though, he had expectations that they'd pay it forward.

This skill-sharing method implemented by Papa has become my understanding of how we can really level the playing field and grow our communities. This is why I talk about growing up in Dreamland.

The way Papa empowered George off the streets, giving him life skills that he could use for the rest of his life, is the way to build and sustain community.

These lessons in particular are woven through the fabric of our AAU program, Team CP3. My family, along with the great coaches and our community, have all built this together. We do what we do in the spirit of Papa's work around giving and connecting with community. We took his model of teaching not just how to fix the car, but imparting life skills while you're at it, and translated it to basketball. The best part of all of this is that the results are the same. You can be teaching people how to fix cars or how to play basketball, but mentoring is mentoring and we're extremely proud of that.

13

THE GAME

- -

Parkland High School, Winston-Salem
Parkland vs. West Forsyth High
November 20, 2002

We started the second half with a substantial double-digit lead, but Coach Laton left me in, keeping his word—as he always did. Apparently, there was talk all around me on the bench and in the stands about how I could beat MJ's scoring record. DG must have told the guys about my plan to honor Papa tonight. Coach Laton became aware of it too and he joined the team in pushing me toward my goal.

I kept glancing over at my dad, who was an assistant coach, and I could see he was as emotional as I was.

Coach Laton, noticing what was happening in the game, asked my dad, "How many more does he need?"

"More what?! Get him out!" Dad had no clue what he was talking about.

I wasn't aware of any side conversations or anything anyone else in the stands was thinking about. I was focused on doing what I needed to do. I couldn't really do anything except play the way Papa would have wanted me to.

And even though I was the one everyone was watching at that point, that night wasn't about me, or the team, or Dad, or the coach—that night was about Papa.

The crowd was screaming, "CP3! CP3!" but I couldn't hear them, and my dad was waving at me, trying to get my attention—but I couldn't pay attention to him, because I was locked in. All I could do was keep playing. I hit a short jumper, another layup, a floater, and then scored again and again and again.

Parkland's defense was lost, confused, visibly defeated. I never really played during a blowout so usually I wouldn't even be in at this point. Normally in this situation, we'd just be about maintaining the lead and getting other teammates some playing time, but that night, I couldn't help it. I was just focused on playing my heart out for Papa. Focusing on that and that only was my coping mechanism. In high school, you didn't put your foot on the neck of a team already down. This game, though, was for Papa; it was different. Bucket after bucket, then there was a whistle. I don't remember who told me or how I found out how many points I had, but somehow in that moment I knew it.

With less than two minutes left, I had scored fifty-nine.

14

THAT MAMBA MENTALITY

EVERYTHING NEGATIVE—PRESSURE, CHALLENGES—
IS ALL AN OPPORTUNITY FOR ME TO RISE.
—KOBE BRYANT

Kobe Bryant and I were almost on the same team. Hell, we actually were for a couple of hours.

How crazy would that have been? Over a decade after the trade wasn't allowed, it's hard not to imagine the "what ifs"? Although it's fun to think about us playing together, I wouldn't change my path for anything, and everything happens for a reason. I know it would have been an unreal experience playing with Kobe. I know that because we both shared an intense relationship and obsession with hard work.

It is a famous NBA story now. We had a deal done for me to be traded to the Lakers from the New Orleans Hornets during the 2010–2011 off-season, but the deal was blocked by the late NBA commissioner David Stern. This never happens, but it did this time because at that time the league owned the Hornets and that was the decision he and the league made. The Lakers were in a really great position to get me and the finances worked out so that the Lakers would have avoided the NBA's luxury tax. I would have been teamed in the backcourt with one of the best basketball players of all time. I can't even imagine how far we could have gone and how dominant we could have been. That wasn't in the cards for me, though, and easy has never been a part of my story. I'm sure you can imagine how frustrating it was to be denied a chance to play with Kobe. We got a taste of it at the 2009 All-Star Game when the two of us on the West teamed up to smack the East. Once that trade didn't work out, I was still crazy excited to get to LA with the Clippers. I had a great, storied, six-year run with the Clippers, including Blake Griffin, DeAndre Jordan, JJ Redick, Jamal Crawford, and Matt Barnes, which was known as the Lob City era. No rim lowering needed over there, you're welcome Dad.

Kobe and I went back years and had some of our fondest memories in 2008, during the Olympics in Beijing. Kobe and I were both early birds so it was always interesting to see which one of us would get to the gym first.

Even at the Olympics, I always wanted to get work in when people were sleeping. I pride myself still on my ability to get up early and get that work in before everyone else even gets their day started. One morning in Beijing, it had to be 5:00 a.m., and I got down to the gym and I already heard some people in there. I couldn't believe it. Who in the world could have beat me? I was usually the one turning on the lights, but now as I was approaching the gym, I started to see who was up outworking everyone else. Of course it was Kobe, and he had already worked up a sweat. This especially struck me because Kobe was a lot older than I was, and he was still working like that. Most players would have thought he didn't have to do that at his age and after all he'd accomplished. He could have slept in and met us there after we warmed up, and he'd earned that respect, but that wasn't Kobe. He stayed hungry. Seeing Kobe in action was a subtle reminder of what my Phoenix Suns coach Monty Williams always says: *"reps remove doubt."* We were proud together as a unit, with Kobe as our leader, to bring back Gold to the USA.

And then when the season rolled around, Kobe and I had to turn around and guard each other. I got to witness Mamba Mentality from the Mamba himself. Seeing him in action, being close enough to absorb his aura, had a way of making you a better player. It's crazy to think about how someone who has accomplished that much was still chasing that next level. I always thought about what could have been. Well, there's another dimension to his game that people never really got to see. A lot of people don't realize, or just never paid attention to it, but Kobe was great at catch and shoot. I imagine if we were backcourt mates, I could have drawn a substantial amount of attention to me, giving Kobe the opportunity to move without the ball, spot up, catch, and knock down shots from anywhere on the court. Trust me, he did this for 20 years without me, but I like to think I could have helped a little bit! I know it would have been crazy, but damn, we never got our shot. Long live the Mamba, we miss you and love you, Bean.

Being a winner requires a ridiculous amount of work. I was trying to explain this to Lil Chris on one of those days when he and one of his friends decided to work out with me. This was a few weeks after our service station visit. We were still feeling that Winston-Salem energy. We were going over a series of shooting drills, and every time the ball rimmed out or he missed, Lil Chris grew angrier and just began to flip out, so I asked, "Whatchu mad for?"

He responded by grabbing the basketball and attempting more shots.

"Are you supposed to make every shot? Like how much time do you put into this?" He just looked at me without an expression on his face. I could tell he was getting frustrated, so I slowed it down. "Listen, I don't care if you don't want to play basketball. If you love basketball and want to be a part of the game, there are more ways to get involved, like scouting, ownership, becoming an NBA executive, an agent, a coach—the possibilities are endless."

For me, the trip back to the station was my attempt to show my kids a reality outside of the one we enjoy, in an effort to strengthen their relationship with hard work—to walk them through the places where Papa got his hands dirty, where CJ and I got dirty too for the bulk of our childhood. Cam is hooping now too so if they both can see the place that molded me, then maybe they can develop their own idea of what working hard really is, their own personal Mamba Mentalities.

Kobe has been quoted as saying, "Trying to be the best version of yourself, that's what the mentality means. It means every day you know you're trying to become better. If your job is to try to be the best basketball player you can be, you have to practice, you have to train as much as you can as often as you can."

I love this quote. You're only as good as your

work ethic—if a guy like Kobe is taking one or two thousand shots a day, then why should he feel okay trusting you with the ball if you're complaining about taking fifty shots a day or not going to practice at all? Kobe worked hard as hell and it showed. He wasn't out there actively trying to embarrass people, it happened because he worked so hard. I drill this into the heads of all players who come through my camps. There's always a guy vying for your job. Are you going to just sit there and let them take it? I keep up this mentality to this day. No one is going to take my job because I'm not working hard enough to keep it.

Winners like Kobe have a laser focus on winning—they hold you accountable, they push you to be the best, and when you think you have reached your best, real winners push you to go even further. The relentless pursuit of winning isn't fun at times, but it for sure can change your life.

I remember being a young NBA player and hearing all the stories about guys like Kobe Bryant and others I looked up to and the amazing, impossible, and inspiring workouts they did. Workouts that scared so many players away—workouts that I learned to run toward. No way in the world was I going to sit around and hear that there's another player out there working harder than I am. Just when I thought I was working hard, I'd ask myself if I could work harder. People who achieve success at really high levels—in sports, in business, or otherwise— are wired differently.

People always ask me what I do differently, and the answer is simple: somewhere along the line, I learned to fall in love with the work. I love practice, I love weight training, I just love being in the gym. And you see that with all the greats in any sport. Success is all about figuring out your own weaknesses, learning how to combat them, and then making that a routine. Papa did this too. I'm pretty sure my grandpa didn't want to wake up at the crack of dawn every day to deal with everyone and anyone and their issues, some who paid and some who didn't, some who were grateful and some who weren't. But he did what had to be done in an effort to take care of everyone. I watched Papa perform daily, and that kind of work ethic seeped into my soul. It's why I'm so proud to be one of the oldest players in the NBA at this moment. I'm not willing to lose my spot in the league because I didn't work hard or look for every edge I could get.

Greatness doesn't just happen to people. It doesn't just sneak up on you. We all have different talents and attributes. Some of us are taller, which has advantages, some are physically gifted, some are incredibly bright; those God-given talents mean nothing without work, and being a hard worker can be taught. Papa directly and indirectly gifted that kind of work ethic to CJ and me every day. It didn't matter what we had going on in our lives, we wanted to be at the top, working and becoming better.

That's where I learned to handle uncertainty, deal with negativity, and conquer people who didn't believe in me. When someone tells me I can't do something, I'm immediately thinking how I can show them that I can. My parents always talk about how I was crazy competitive even back as a kid. I grew up being the kind of guy who actually thrived when the odds were stacked against me. Being disrespected or counted out forces me to take my game to the next level. When I got to OKC, there was a graphic on ESPN that said our team had a .02 percent chance of making the playoffs. I took a screenshot and kept it in my phone, just to remember that somebody was trying to count me out. And guess what: we made the playoffs! Being counted out isn't new to me, and I also truly appreciate those who believe in me like I believe in myself. This reminds me of Coach recruiting me to Wake when UNC was counting me out. This mentality is there for everyone if you want it enough and if you care enough about what you're doing. It could be brake pads or getting back on defense, grinding and putting in the work will always pay off.

15

TEAM CP3, ANOTHER KIND OF FAMILY

- -

FIFTEEN SECONDS OF COURT TIME, THAT'S
HOW LONG CJ AND I PLAYED TOGETHER

Sometimes I think about my teenage days, back when I played AAU basketball for the Kappa Magic. My team won the National 17U AAU title and I even was named tournament MVP as an undersized point guard. The whole experience became a huge part of who I am as a player now and why I knew, once I was able, that I needed to give as many young players as possible an AAU experience and the lessons that come with it. It's so special that I can relive my AAU days through my teams today and try to give them as much as I can.

Somewhere in the world, there is a guy trying to rank first-graders. Even though I know basketball will end up being more than a fun sport for some, it's important at that age to focus on love of the game and the platform it gives you versus all of the hype and highlight reels you see. I got the innocent opportunity to fall in love with the game while training with my dad and playing one-on-one against CJ. It's a little harder on kids today because as soon as their talent is recognized, people who want to take advantage come out of the woodwork, from every angle, hungry with their own agenda. AAU basketball used to be so pure, but now there are a lot of other factors at play and not everyone's motives are solid.

The perception of AAU basketball ideally would be hardworking kids blessed with the opportunity to try their talents out against people in different states and sometimes on the other side of the world. But on the flip side, AAU is big business, and as we all know, with big money comes challenges. All of the potential drama and craziness is one of the main reasons why I'm so involved in my program. That, and I love paying it forward. I have been extremely blessed in my career, and I just love helping develop those I see potential in.

Lifting up the collective is why I took my role as president of the Players Association so seriously. I knew there was real work to be done. There are players who end up in bad spots because they are missing resources, mentorship, and certain protections to set them up for success, both personally and financially, for their post-NBA career future. I hate hearing stories about guys I admire not being able to afford a life they deserve given what they gave to the game. I wanted to change that. Basketball can give you a lot professionally, on every level.

My nickname is CP3 because me, my brother, and my dad all have the same initials: CEP. My dad is CP1: Charles Edward Paul, my brother is CP2:

Charles Edward Paul Jr., and I am the third, CP3: Christopher Emmanuel Paul. And my number in the NBA is and has always been 3. Naturally then, our team for AAU was called Team CP3—to represent our family. Our organization mirrors the closeness we share in our family. Of course, my mom, the former banker, does all the accounting and handles the paperwork, just like she did at Jones Chevron, as that is her area of expertise. To this day, she still books all the flights and hotels and handles other details for my AAU team as well as managing all my foundation's activities. CJ has an incredible eye for talent and is always a mentor for the kids. My father, who used to coach, is a mentor, spending time and energy to make sure these young men get everything they need to be successful. Together they all do an amazing, hands-on job continuing to grow our program in the right direction. My parents also educate other parents to let them know how AAU programs work, and what to expect if their kid plays in our program. They also give advice to our AAU kids on how to potentially make it into the league, and they serve as mentors for families in the NBA. Every year, they speak to the families of players getting drafted. When people think of the NBA family, my parents have always been there to be a resource. My dad is also a leader with the NBA fathers. They feel it's so important as a group of predominantly Black men to show a great example of being an active and present father. I find this to be very important because very rarely are the fathers talked about in such a positive light in the NBA community.

Team CP3, our AAU team, is also very competitive and requires a huge time commitment—and it's hard for some young men and women, especially the parents and the families. Some young people think they're into it until they get hit with the rigorous work and mandatory conditioning and realize that it's not for them, which is totally okay. The main goal of the program isn't to mold future NBA or WNBA superstars or draft prospects, it's really to mold good humans with high character and strong work ethics, and hopefully give them a chance to play at the next level. We want to mold leaders on and off the court.

We are in the business of creating a strong, healthy, and competitive basketball family who understands the value of education, hard work, and positivity. We do want to educate families, especially those in tough situations. It can be pretty jarring to all of a sudden see a lot of money being thrown around a young kid. And as a parent, you invest a lot in your kids and you just want to make sure it's handled right.

The landscape of AAU is ever changing and the cost to compete continues to rise every year. I invest in youth sports because it's where I learned leadership, work ethic, how to be a team player, and other skills that stretch far beyond the basketball court. If you are interested in a career in sports, getting that exposure from AAU gives you what you might not otherwise get if you can't afford a well-known prep school, or because your high school team doesn't attract scouts. Beyond a chance of making it to the pros, my family wants to give our kids a chance to get a great education and earn a college scholarship. That's the biggest accomplishment from our team—being able to set kids up for college. We try to instill a sense of responsibility, belonging, and so many more teachings from Papa.

Social media has also had a powerful effect on

recruiting as basketball has become more global. Student athletes from anywhere and everywhere are uploading videos to YouTube, showing their best highlights, and gaining attention from the top coaches whom you thought you were going to impress over the summer.

Another means of basketball development I feel passionately about is elevating HBCU programs, which usually lack the funding that a place like Wake Forest has to build a top-level college basketball program. A goal of mine has been and still is to have some top talent go to HBCUs and raise awareness and funds to get them to develop to that level.

Players on the AAU circuit dream of making it to the pros and that's hard as hell. There are millions of super-talented basketball players all over the world competing to be one of 450 NBA players. And each year there's a draft, so there is a very limited number of positions. We strive to prepare our athletes for the league or college as well as life beyond.

All our coaches serve, and their commitment travels far beyond the basketball court. Our teams' coaches are mentors to their players, strive to teach them more than just about the game of basketball but about discipline, respect, and responsibility. We teach our kids about having a strong community, what that looks like, and the idea of understanding our social responsibilities—giving back to the community that molded them. We also share the soft skills needed to make that happen—the kind of soft skills that so many young Black men and women aren't always granted the opportunity to learn. Like Papa said, get comfortable with being uncomfortable, and I always share that with my AAU kids.

Education is important to me, but finishing something I started is everything to me, which is why I vowed to finish my degree. Though I started at Wake and am grateful for my education and time there, I decided that I am going to finish my degree at Winston-Salem State, an HBCU. I love the idea that I can marry both worlds that I am a part of and can tell both stories.

Once you become a part of our grassroots program, you are a part of our family for life. I truly love that the kids affiliated with Team CP3 always come back to help out, teach, coach, and show love. Nobody probably appreciates it more than the kids. You can see one of my teams at Peach Jam and it's not crazy to see Harry Giles, Theo Pinson, or another former player there cheering the guys on. We have about a dozen NBA guys who came through the program. They're all great guys who will do so much in their lives. It's funny that I've been in the NBA for so long that I play against kids from my program who are still in the habit of calling me *Coach*. One of our success stories, actually the first Team CP3 player to make it to the NBA, was Reggie Bullock.

Reggie is family and I love him to death. I knew him since he was a kid, and I honestly get emotional thinking about him losing two sisters to violence, one in 2014 and another in 2019. His story, coming out of a small town in Kinston, North Carolina, is something special. And what's beautiful is that Reggie works so hard at making the world better for other people, from the activism he participates in for the LBGTQ+ community, to how he is always setting a positive example for other players. Reggie Bullock is the pure representation of what it means to be a fighter—from his obvious resiliency, to his journey so far in the league.

I'm proud that Reggie was a product of our program. Beyond him, many other players from our program have gone on to have professional careers in and outside of basketball. And the fact that so many players who are products of our program still stay in touch with our family even if they're not in the NBA means we're doing what we're supposed to be doing.

Team CP3 is a family, and that theme is woven through everything we do. When I say *family,* I tap into that idea that I got from Papa, centered around just being truly present.

All these AAU roads lead back to Papa's teachings and sensibility. The reason we invest in grassroots basketball is to show Papa's messages to as many people as possible: to help people out when you see them in a tough spot, lift as you climb, and always remember that you are only as good as the people around you. That is what community is: us helping us.

The beauty of community is that it holds you up and supports you through every aspect of your life. I still remember when I made one of the most difficult decisions of my career, which was leaving the LA Clippers. I loved being in LA, loved my teammates and my family had become more than comfortable being in Los Angeles.

We had so much fun those years on the Clippers, but we had our challenges, just like any other team. Communication sometimes became an issue. That's not news. Everyone speculates about what happened or who said what to whom, but it wasn't all that dramatic. We still could have won, regardless of any perceived issues. We're professionals and would have put any differences aside to win, and I know everyone on that team wanted to win. Despite any of those challenges, we always thought we were next up to win it all and regret that we never did. Doc Rivers, our coach at the Clippers, always would say to win at anything you need "a lot of work and a little bit of luck." I believe that to be true. You never know when something is going to break for the other team. The reality is when you play a game for a living, luck is going to play a factor.

You just have to work your ass off and be ready when luck presents itself to you.

I would also say that there's a challenge to living in LA. It's a massive city. People live in different areas, far apart, have lots of things to do and their own agendas. When I first got there, it was a culture shock coming from New Orleans, where it was so much simpler being in a smaller city. In both scenarios, there were efforts to hang out, get to know each other's families, have the opportunity to build with one another and use experiences off the court to further our connections on the court. Every team I've been a part of has had its own identity. My Thunder team was great as well, because everyone counted us out, yet every night we knew we could beat anyone. The great thing about playing for the Phoenix Suns now is that there are guys at different stages in their career that bring different things to the table.

No matter where I am or what team I'm a part of, I try to keep the main thing the main thing. I watch games religiously, every night, no matter how many games are on. I study. I've been doing that for my entire career. I study to see what I did wrong, where I'm helping my teammates best, and how we can improve. I do this every day. Anyone who knows me knows I get so excited to watch games every night. Coach Monty and I text at times during games and don't even have to address what game we're talking about. We just both talk about plays that we know the other is watching.

This obsession with the game led me to want to try and make it to Houston despite our comfort level in LA. I hated how this process of figuring out my professional life versus my personal life affected my family and relationships. As hard as that debate was, ultimately we made the tough decision to leave the Clippers.

Papa and my parents always showered me in unconditional love, despite any work situations or other things they had going on, and my kids deserve the same energy. This is how I felt then and still feel to this day. I knew I could do better if I was in the right basketball situation. My decision to stay or leave had to be based on being the best version of my basketball self so that I could be the best version of my overall self for my family.

I didn't have to process this on my own because, again, I had community, so I reached out to my good friend and mentor, Jay-Z. Jay had invited me to the studio to listen to some of the tracks on his upcoming album *4:44*. I was documenting my upcoming free agency process and how I was making that decision, so we brought a camera to film the conversation. This moment was really special because initially I brought the camera to have content for my own personal archives, but it ended up becoming the first official project for my production company, Ohh Dip!!!

It was a dope moment for me and CJ as we arrived at the studio and found ourselves with no I.D., Guru, and Jay. We ended up spending hours just talking about life and how certain decisions impact and affect everything. We all know that Jay had long ago earned the reputation of a mogul and person who continues to make really savvy business decisions. Our conversation was about all things basketball, family, and life. I began to lay all of the pros and cons that I was weighing in order to make this difficult decision. A lot weighed on me: there was a financial aspect to this decision; the emotional part of leaving the Clippers; then, most importantly, how this decision could affect the people who are closest to me.

"That's what you really have to think about. Do you want to uproot your family?" Jay said, taking a long pause, hitting on my biggest concern. "Your happiness, that is worth everything. If you come back here, you shouldn't be playing for nothing but your happiness."

Beyond my wife and kids, I would have to up-root my brother, CJ, and his family as well, because that's just sort of what we do. Even though my brother wanted me to be completely happy so that I could perform at the highest level, his happiness mattered to me just as much. It wasn't just CJ's family I thought about. There were so many people connected to my basketball career in LA, and I had to consider them all—my chef, trainers, doctors, security, and more. Not to mention all of their families—I had to worry about them too.

"My gut tells me, I know you, and you aren't going to be happy playing basketball," Jay continued. "An extra fifty million will not change your life. It doesn't matter if you get a hundred and fifty, get two hundred, it's the same thing. You're going to ride the same plane, you're going to take the same trips, but you're not going to be happy if you're not playing the way you want to play."

And even though I wasn't quite sure where I was going, it felt great to be able to talk to Jay and other mentors I had, like one of my closest friends and Disney CEO Bob Iger, about such a huge decision. Mentors like that can say the things that you need to hear so that you can move forward. While actually making the decision was hard, the most difficult part was yet to come: breaking the news to my kids. Cam was so young that this wasn't going to affect her too drastically. She probably didn't even truly understand that I played in the NBA at that time. But I knew I needed to let her know anyway, because that's my baby girl.

"Cam, Daddy may be moving to another team," I told her while she was sitting on my lap. "Houston. What do you think about going to Houston?"

She stared back with a big, sweet, innocent, but slightly confused grin. "Is Mommy coming?" Cam responded.

"Of course Mommy is coming," I answered. And that was all she needed to hear from me. Cam was in.

And there was Lil Chris. Breaking it to him was the absolute hardest part, because he had become so comfortable in LA, and had started establishing real friendships. He had made a lot of friends and loved our neighborhood and even the school he went to. I was scared that the news of us picking up and starting over was going to crush him, but it was a conversation we had to have. I'll never forget seeing him read the ESPN ticker on the TV in my office the morning that the trade went through. He was devastated that we were leaving LA.

So I found him in the house and pulled him in close so we could talk about it. I could see the disappointment all over his face as he imagined losing all his friends in the blink of an eye. I extended my hand to wipe the tears that instantly began to pour down his face.

"Daddy, do I have to go?" he asked. "I like it here."

"I need you, Chris," I told him, holding back tears myself, pulling him in even closer and wrapping my arms around his small shoulders. "I need y'all! I know I can't perform the way I'm expected to on the court without y'all being there. I need you with me, man." And Lil Chris responded with a strong, "Okay," because he knew that I needed him.

One thing that my parents provided was consistency; we always had the same house, in the same neighborhood, and were surrounded by family and the same group of people, and that was our life. It wasn't hard for us to define community because it was always there, right in front of our faces. My children have had a completely different reality because I play basketball for a living. My job has required me to move and disrupt my family a few times. What we try and keep consistent, though, is the sense of community that Papa introduced me to—building a strong support system made up of family and friends. As parents, Jada and I are charged with the difficult task of taking our unique reality and figuring out ways to create normalcy for our kids. We certainly do our best, but sometimes we truly wish it could be easier.

Building that kind of community can be difficult when you have to move from town to town; so when I was traded to the Oklahoma City Thunder in the summer of 2019, we made another extremely difficult decision. It was time to give my kids that consistency that I had and have my family move back to LA. For the first time in my career, I was going to be away from my kids and living by myself. The same holds true now that I play in Phoenix—though luckily that's a much closer flight. I fly home as much as I can on off days to get in every minute I can, but I have some really tough moments where I just need my family. This is why I said earlier that Jada is the most important part of my family. I know it's not easy on her with me being gone, but she is the rock that keeps everyone together.

16

A GLORIOUS DAY

- - - - - - - - - - - - - - - - - - -

NEVER DELAY GRATITUDE.

—COACH SKIP PROSSER

Thursday, November 14, 2002, is a day that I'll never forget as long as I live.

It was the day I was signing my letter of intent to play basketball at Wake Forest, a school that was close to home but represented how far I'd grown as a basketball player and as a person. I felt the sum of so much hard work as I gripped the pen to make it official. This was everything I had dreamed of—playing college ball. This day was not just huge for me, but for my family too, especially Papa. I think this was the biggest day of my life at that point. CJ even drove back about two and a half hours from USC Upstate to be there for me. Papa, wearing his dress clothes and church shoes of course, was right there watching me, beaming with pride. He even had his old Wake Forest hat perched like a snug crown on his bald head.

I'm sure you've seen high school kids commit to colleges to play sports. They usually have five or six hats with different schools on them to make it dramatic and then pick the one that they're going to attend. Sometimes even before they sign the letter of intent they know all along, sometimes even months before, what school they are going to. I didn't do any of that, though. I just signed the letter. Some press was there, but it wasn't a circus by any means. Right after I signed, Papa took his beloved Wake Forest hat right off his head and gave it to me to put on. I still remember how it smelled like that foamy soap from the service station and those damn cigarettes.

He pulled me close and whispered in my ear, "Christopher Emmanuel Paul"—he never called me that—"I will remember this day for the rest of my life."

That's when it all finally hit me. I was there, wearing Papa's hat, making the biggest decision of my life. I still get emotional today just thinking about that moment.

We took pictures, shook everyone's hands, and that was it. CJ hopped back in the car to make his drive back to USCU.

While everybody else went their separate ways after the signing, Papa and I went to a preseason game at Wake Forest that night. Just me and him. I don't remember who they played against, I was just happy to be in the building for the first time officially as a Demon Deacon. Nobody else went with us, which, looking back, was actually uncommon for a game. I know my mom was working a second shift, Dad had been cleaning out office spaces for extra money, but usually someone else from our family would have been with us. Not that night, though; it was just me, Papa, and the game. We had a great time, excited to know that I too would be at Wake playing so close to home. I'd be wearing that #3 jersey with PAUL on the back next year, and Papa would be on the sidelines. I'd have to get him a brand-new Wake Forest hat and maybe he'd even put on a #3 Demon Deacon jersey over his blue work suit. One thing that wouldn't change, though, is that he'd have on the best church shoes his money could buy. We worked so hard for all of this through all the AAU games, the JV drama, and the backyard battles with CJ. It all had prepared me for this moment, and I was going to shine just like Papa's shoes.

Pride just spilled out from Papa—he was so full of pure joy that other people probably thought he was about to hoop at Wake, too. I adjusted the old, bent Wake Forest cap to my head—the smell of smoke so strong it was like it had been dipped in tobacco. Even though I don't smoke cigarettes and didn't want Papa to smoke them, I loved it because it smelled like home. The game came to an end, and we made our way out.

"You ready for next year?" Papa said as we loaded up his car. I closed the door, sank into the huge leather seats of his Lincoln that smelled just like the cap, and snapped on my seat belt.

"College is a whole different level, Papa. I have to lock in even more to get ready."

"Yes, you will. Don't worry about that," Papa said as we exited the lot and cruised. "You have a year to prepare."

"I'm not taking any days off," I assured him. "If it wasn't so late already tonight I'd start training now!"

"It's been an eventful day." Papa laughed as we pulled up to the house. "I'm proud of you, Chris. Get some rest."

"You too, Papa," I said, adjusting my new-old Wake Forest cap. "You too, and thank you. For everything. Love you."

Papa nodded, pulled off, and I yelled behind him, "Call me when you get home!"

He hit the horn in affirmation, and I waved again as he continued down the block. I had no idea that that would be the last time I would ever see him.

17

BUILD A LEADER

FOLLOWERS PLAY CHECKERS,
LEADERS PLAY CHESS.
—AUTHOR UNKNOWN

Thinking about signing day and Papa, and how much he's missed out on, has me remembering another man gone too soon. My coach, Skip Prosser, made a huge and lasting impact on my life in the short time we were together.

During my first few months at Wake Forest,

there were a lot of new things coming at me. Some of them I expected, like eating way too much unhealthy food. I swear we lived at IHOP my freshman year. It was right off campus next to a Pizza Hut, another spot we hit up a bunch, but it was IHOP where we all really did some damage. I'd always order the pigs in a blanket—two sausages rolled up into two pancakes. Even though I don't eat that way anymore, I can still confidently say it was fire. Going into college, you hear all about late-night junk food runs, and that definitely was part of my first year on campus. Also new to me was dealing with how I stood out around campus as a member of the basketball team. Wake has the typical college quad and what we called the Pit, our dining hall. Walking around with everybody knowing who you are would take some getting used to. Students, faculty, and alumni were all so passionate about Wake Forest basketball that I felt that weight and fascination sometimes even just walking into a classroom. It was the first time in my life that I got a glimpse of public life—for people to know who you are and hearing them go crazy over it. Since I committed to Wake as a junior and was from Winston-Salem, my whole senior year of high school, Wake fans were following me everywhere. You hear a lot about how college athletes don't always get the full college experience, especially guys that only play for one season. I feel really lucky because in my two years at Wake, I really felt like I got a traditional college experience. We went to parties all the time—nothing crazy, just college parties—but I got to see what all of the other students experienced. I also got a glimpse into Greek life at Wake. The sorority Delta Zeta had their famous sweetheart ceremony, and they picked me, which was interesting, but cool. Basically being a sweetheart just meant they'd come by and bring some cookies or things like that all the time.

I appreciated being able to have a relatively normal experience at Wake, but there were some things I'll admit I didn't see coming. One of those was how hard Coach Prosser pushed academics. He cared about what grades we got as much as how well we played basketball. My folks absolutely loved this. I was playing really well and that was why I was at Wake in the first place, but my academic success was a priority for all of us. My mother has countless stories that start with us going to Kinko's in the middle of the night because I was up trying to complete a project and left it until the last minute, sorta how it's been writing this book. I had a lot going on with basketball, but I still had to make sure I finished what I needed to for school. No matter how good my game was, if my grades weren't right, then I wasn't going to be able to play. Coach assured my family that I was going to get a great education and build powerful relationships that extended far past the basketball court, and he delivered on that.

Coach also told my family that he saw me as more than a basketball player; he saw me as a great student and person who loved my community. He promised to help enhance all of that during my time at Wake Forest. Of all the places that tried to recruit me, Wake Forest was the one college that really stood out in terms of building a bond with me as a person. Coach and his recruiting team made me feel like they cared about me, and that was special. The most beautiful part is that they kept that same energy my entire time there. It's important for me to say this because sometimes you hear nightmare stories from other players about how schools did anything and everything in their power to get them to play there, but spent no time developing them outside of basketball. That was not my experience.

I used to come into Coach Prosser's office as a freshman, and he would ask, "Chris, how are you doing today?"

Not thinking anything of it, I'd always reply, "I'm good, Coach."

"You are *well*, Chris. Well."

Years later, I find myself correcting people the same way. He always wanted his players to be able to compete on and off the court, and he knew language matters. It especially mattered for him to help us combat stereotypes around us as athletes.

Coach loved to tell us "Integrity is everything," every chance he got. My teammates and I always talked about how he'd correct our grammar, imparting his mantras—also known as Prosser-isms or Skip-isms—to us. Some of my favorites were, "If you can't be on time, be early," and "Don't be a three-to-six guy, be a six-to-three guy," and "Never delay gratitude."

All the lessons I knew that I needed to live by weighed on me. I was a top recruit and a McDonald's All-American. Josh Howard, a hometown hero, was drafted into the NBA right before my freshman year, so I had some pretty big shoes to fill as they had just won the ACC Championship and Josh was named ACC Player of the Year. The starting point guard was a junior named Taron Downey, our team captain from Oxford, North Carolina. His backcourt mate was my boy J Gray, who was a sophomore from Charlotte. I was eager to learn but also to try and earn a starting spot. I had never come off the bench before and was hoping I didn't end up having to in college.

I worked my butt off in practice and was dedicated to showing what I could do. I played defense and made sure they saw that I knew how to run an offense, but Coach Prosser never said anything about me starting. Our first game was to be played at the legendary Madison Square Garden in New York City against The University of Memphis, and I was ready. They had a senior point guard named Antonio Burks, who was nice. A few weeks before we went to the Big Apple, Taron got a case of appendicitis. With him being out, Coach P asked me to step up and start. I thought this would just be temporary.

Game time rapidly approached, and Taron had fully recovered. I thought I did what I had to do and paired well with J Gray, but I could have accepted it if Coach decided to start Taron. This was different from my JV/varsity experience at West Forsyth. After all, I was a freshman and had a whole lot of time to learn the game. Taron worked out with the team, and at the end of practice, Coach gathered us all up and announced, "Chris is going to be the starting point guard."

A whirlwind of emotions came over me as I prepared to officially start my journey as a college basketball player. I remember that night, November 13, 2003, when I felt the presence of my best friend once again. I was standing in the historic locker room of the heralded Madison Square Garden and had begun to put on my brand-new bright white uniform, with the capitalized letters of PAUL on my back, for the very first time—a bittersweet feeling it was, which brought tears to my eyes.

It was a blessing, but also put some extra weight on my shoulders, being a freshman and a starter. Most people on Division I college teams were the best in whatever city or state they came from, and that was my competition now. I loved going up against vets with experience to prove myself. I worked hard and did everything I had to do to make sure my team won and that was all that mattered.

We beat Memphis in my first game, and I had a pretty good game, especially for a person making college debut. All the work paid off; I felt like my starting job was pretty secure. A part of me knows that I got lucky things broke my way—but as we've been saying, luck happens when preparation meets opportunity. A part of me also knows that the things I learned at the service station, like being relentless, confident, and trusting my skills, allowed me to keep the job once the opportunity was in front of me.

Another Prosser-ism I loved, one I actually still use to this day in my AAU program and basketball camps, is his "ABCs of Life" saying.

Character is the necessary ingredient in being a strong leader and making sure you are doing everything in your power to take care of the guys on your team. I played eighty games for Coach between my two years in college and started in seventy-nine of them. The only time I didn't start had nothing to do with an injury, academics, or how I played ball. It was about accountability.

Mardy Collins was Temple's senior point guard, and I was looking forward to battling with him. Eric "Big E" Williams, our center, was my roommate on this particular road trip. Big E was also a McDonald's All-American. He grew up in Chicago but eventually moved to North Carolina after his parents separated, where he played high school ball. Big E was always cool, and laid-back.

He had a unique sense of humor and a few dope tattoos, most of which he drew himself.

Usually on road trips, our time was pretty scheduled, and we went from the bus to the hotel to the gym to the bus to travel back home. We had almost no time to see the cities we played in, but that wasn't important because these were business trips. This one particular trip to Philly, though, was different. We ended up having a little more downtime, so being a nineteen-year-old college kid, I took that opportunity. My longtime friend Rich Paul decided to pull up to Philly for this particular game. We were going to go by the Mitchell & Ness Store to check it out. The store was famous for its selection of sports jerseys. Everybody was obsessed with those jerseys. And we all wore them three sizes too big, with baggy jeans and whatever kind of Jordans or Air Force Ones were fresh at that moment. If you came up around the same time as I did, you know Mitchell & Ness was the place for throwbacks. They had everything from a Magic Johnson Lakers home game uniform to an Isaiah Thomas All-Star Game jersey to the Houston Oilers' Warren Moon and

Philadelphia Eagles' Randall Cunningham jerseys. That store was a sports fan's paradise. They didn't just have throwbacks either. They had all new stuff like local hero Allen Iverson's jersey and anything else you could imagine. Unfortunately, it was also all too expensive for a college kid from Winston-Salem.

We hit the store, but I didn't grab anything. Just seeing the collection of jerseys was a huge win for me.

Allen Iverson was my favorite basketball player at the time; I shared that fandom with my mom. A six-foot, one-inch guard that was beyond fearless, he was ready to challenge anyone and everyone on both ends of the court. A few years earlier, I had gotten my hair braided in zigzags just like his and went right to bed with a do-rag on so my pops wouldn't see, because I knew my dad would make me take them out. And of course, Dad saw, and before I knew it, those braids were gone.

While I was in Philly for the game, I got a chance to meet up and see A.I. This was a moment I'll never forget.

I was having such a great time and got a full taste of Philly. I got back to the team hotel after an amazing experience with Rich and AI. We then had a team meeting, and it was back to my normally scheduled program.

I was getting ready to lie down for a nap, as I always do on game day, and said to Big E, "I'm going to call downstairs and get us a wake-up call."

"I'm not tired, C, don't even worry about that. I'm not going to sleep. I'll wake you up to get ready."

Big E was still wide wake watching *Dragon Ball Z*. Dude loved *Dragon Ball Z*. He watched it faithfully, and it was easy for him to do so, because every student that attended Wake Forest was given a laptop.

"Yoooo, please don't forget to wake me up," I reiterated. "I don't want to oversleep."

In our hotel room, my bed was closest to the door, and Big E's bed was on the left side of the room. Most basketball players in college and the pros like to take a nap before the game and we all know the importance of that alarm clock. I had no reason to second-guess Big E and he said he's got us, so I got comfortable in bed and went to sleep.

It seemed like as soon as I closed my eyes, I was awakened by a terrible booming followed by a series of more. BOOM, BOOM, BOOM, BOOM, BOOM, BOOM, BOOM, BOOM, BOOM!

It sounded like police officers were trying to bust through the door. I immediately jumped up, disoriented, and called over to Big E, who was stretched out on the bed, knocked out with the laptop on, *Dragon Ball Z* characters screaming.

"E, get up!" I yelled. "Yo!"

"What y'all doin?!" our assistant coach Chris Mack shouted through the door. "We're waiting for you!"

"Here we come," I responded, panicking, noticing we were late. "Big E, get up!"

Big E and I hustled our things together and bolted down to the lobby as quickly as we could. The whole team was already on the bus, packed up and ready to go. It was and still is one of the most embarrassing moments of my playing career. I'm never late and being late was a cardinal sin to Coach Prosser. Remember? "If you can't be on time, be early." I had broken a Skip-ism! What was worse was that I knew I'd disappointed him.

I looked on the bus, turning my head left, trying to catch eyes with Coach Prosser before I came all the way on. And I'll never forget how Coach Prosser was sitting in the first seat, with a look cold as ice. The walk from the three stairs you climb to get on the bus and then past Coach, who wouldn't even look at me, felt like a ten-mile hike. Big E shared the moment with me, but it wasn't the same for him. I was supposed to be the team leader, even as a freshman; I was supposed to do everything right after having earned that starting spot. I knew better. We were only a couple of minutes late, but late is late. Leaders should always be early and the team cannot see me being irresponsible or looking like I think I have my own set of rules. That can contribute to terrible team chemistry.

I have had the blessing of being the leader my whole life; it just came naturally to me because of the example set by Papa. On the football field, I was the quarterback, and on basketball teams, I have always been the point guard. I've always been the guy when we play pickup games at the Y to keep the score, and keep everyone organized. I was the National Basketball Players Association president; I was class president in high school and worked on planning our reunions. I think Papa just showed me what it meant to lead through service. Being late is a bad leadership trait. I don't strive to be perfect, I just want to be respectful of others' time and energy. So being late, that hurt.

Coach Prosser, who normally always had something to say to me, was as quiet as a church mouse. I knew he was mad, I could feel it, and I really wanted to make it up to him. I thought maybe I could apologize to him, have a great game, and everything be cool. We got to the arena and Coach Prosser started going over plays on the whiteboard. Then he wrote out the starting lineup. My name wasn't on the whiteboard. I was sick. Big E and I were benched, and letting down my teammates crushed me. Thank God we won the game or I don't know what I would have done. I felt like I hadn't just let my team down, but I'd let my family and myself down. That was the last thing anyone needed.

Trent Strickland, small forward and lockdown defender, ended up being the star that day. Coach Prosser was quoted in *The Washington Post* after the game: "I don't think we win the game without Trent Strickland."

"Trent Strickland is a winner. He stepped up big for us on both ends of the court. We have to give him a game ball," I added. "He gets the emotion going for us."

I was so happy for Trent and that we pulled that game out. The *C* stands for character, and I will also include community. The role community plays in sports is something that I try to pay attention to. Papa always taught me that it was about the group, the collective. I fell short that day, but my community just kept going. We celebrated Trent because he deserved it; we always celebrated our teammates' accomplishments and this was no different.

Coach could have yelled at me, cursed me out, and embarrassed me for not being the leader he knew I was, but instead, he just gave me the silent treatment. He wasn't mad, he was just disappointed, and that was *way* worse. The good news is, I learned from it and ended up never making the same mistake again. Big E had to find another roommate for the next road trip, and I made sure to set my own damn alarm every time I took a pregame nap.

It's funny how you can know someone your whole life and they don't necessarily have an impact on the way you think, how you move, or conduct business, but the short time Coach Prosser and I spent in close contact made an everlasting impact on me. That's something only the best of the best coaches can achieve.

Coach will forever be a Wake Forest legend. During his time at the school, he helped increase game attendance and played a significant role in developing our wild student section known as the Screamin' Demons. And, we had the first number-one ranking in the school's history. Most importantly, Coach understood the value of education and the role it plays in changing the lives of young people and their communities. Coach knew all of us weren't going to make it to the NBA but understood that everyone on his team had an opportunity to get a college degree, better themselves, and then use that education to open doors for others. Every senior Coach mentored earned a four-year degree. That's unheard of. That's just one of the reasons Coach is so special and unfortunately, we lost him before he could affect so many more guys.

Coach loved to go for runs. He always started his morning or afternoon with a jog, whenever he could fit it in; trust me, he barely missed a day. On July 26, 2007, after Coach Prosser finished a run, he made his way over to his office, where he sat down on his couch and had a massive heart attack. Coach was found by one of his staff members who worked in basketball ops, Mrs. Heflin, and was immediately rushed over to Wake Forest University Baptist Medical Center, where he was pronounced dead.

Coach Prosser was only fifty-six years old.

I was completely devastated by the news. I still vividly remember the day that I found out Coach passed away. I was in New York at the Waldorf Astoria. We were having a huge NBA negotiation that involved the owners, players' union, and league officials. I was there to speak on behalf of the players when I got a phone call from my former Assistant Coach Jeff Battle.

"He's lying here. He's dead, man. He's dead," Coach Battle said. "He's dead, man."

"What?" I responded. "Who?"

"Coach P. He's not breathing. He's not breathing," Coach Battle continued. "Coach P!"

"What you mean?"

The phone went silent. Shortly thereafter the news spread, and I still feel broken apart to this day about his passing, but I am thankful that I have the memories, his teachings, and am able to be a part of the Wake Forest legacy he created. In that moment, learning that he had died, I kept thinking back to one of my favorite Prosser-isms: *"Never delay gratitude."*

I'm blessed to say that I got so many chances to tell Coach P how much I cared about him and to thank him for the impact he had on my life. Tomorrows aren't promised. Papa taught me that, which ultimately helped me become the kind of person who tries not to take anything for granted.

If you love and appreciate someone, then never *delay gratitude,* because they deserve it.

I'll never forget being at Coach Prosser's funeral, because he was like a father figure to so many guys who loved and respected him—and they all showed up. My teammate at the time on the Hornets, David West, and future Hornet James Posey, came as they both had played for Coach Prosser at Xavier. A bunch of other Wake Forest and Xavier guys also attended. I was one of the people asked to speak about Coach on behalf of some of the guys. It was an honor that I remain grateful for today.

I prepared my words and remember being caught off guard when I spotted the former Pittsburgh Steelers coach Bill Cowher in the crowd among the Wake Forest athletes and famous faces who all loved Coach Prosser.

"Man, you just don't know how excited Coach would be to see you," I said to Coach Bill Cowher, "because he was a Pittsburgh guy to the core. He loved Pittsburgh to death. Everything, like a lot of our practices and games would start off with what the Steelers did in the game the night before!" I still don't know if Cowher and Coach P knew each other personally, but it was so dope for him to be there in that moment honoring Coach P.

I'll forever be thankful to Coach Prosser and pray that he will always rest in power.

18

IT TAKES A VILLAGE
FAMILY HELPING FAMILY

- - - - - - - - - - - - - - - - - -

DON'T MARRY YOUR CAREER AND
DATE YOUR FAMILY.
—KEVIN HART

Nowadays, it's really popular for people to throw around terms like *self-made* or say, "I did it all by myself with no help!" They're trippin'. I understand the notion of committing to work when everyone else is asleep, but nobody gets there alone. For starters, one can't be "self-made"; you're only here because of your parents or whoever had a hand in raising you, and you need that tribe to mold and shape you. The reality is, the further you get in life and the more successful you become, the more you need to rely on others. Sometimes that help will come even from the most unlikely places.

My sophomore year at Wake Forest was nothing short of amazing. For starters, we were ranked number one nationally for the first time in Demon Deacon history. I had really big games against Duke, and had a twenty-three- and a twenty-six-point game against North Carolina—in a time when the ACC was one of the most competitive conferences in college basketball. We made it to the NCAA tournament as the number two seed, beat Chattanooga, but then unfortunately lost to West Virginia in the second round. I finished the season being named First Team Consensus All-American and on ESPN's Academic All-American team. After only two seasons as a Demon Deacon, I ended up with 948 points, 395 assists, and 160 steals, good enough for eighth all-time in school history in assists and seventh all time in steals. As much as I loved Wake and part of me really wanted to finish all four years there, the NBA was calling, and I had to answer.

Once I signed with my agent, I ended up getting ready for the draft with a well-known trainer, Idan Ravin. He earned the nickname "the Hoops Whisperer" as he was one of the best of the best to prep guys for the workout process before getting drafted. He never played professional basketball, period, but still was able to train guys at the highest level. What's interesting about him is that he's a lawyer by trade who at some point in his career became unhappy with practicing law. While living in San Diego, he began coaching Little League teams. As a coach, Idan created all kinds of crazy regimens and drills for his young players and watched their performance improve across the board. His reputation for making players better has become the stuff of legend. Idan ascended from Little League coach to highly sought-after NBA trainer, who has worked with names like Carmelo Anthony and Gilbert Arenas, to name a couple.

Coming out of Wake Forest as a sophomore, I needed to be as prepared as I could and that's what led me to Idan. After declaring for the draft, I packed my bags and moved to Alexandria, Virginia, by the Key Bridge, near Washington, D.C., where Idan was originally from and was located at the time. By the time I arrived in Virginia, I already felt great about all of the recommendations from coaches and fellow players telling me that no one could get me ready for the draft like Idan, and they were right.

We met every day at a Christian school, National Cathedral, with the plan of spending about two hours per session. Idan had me running drills on drills on drills that had me tired as hell. The workouts were no joke—they consisted of me running through all sorts of combinations of cones, between the legs, between the legs cross, and behind the back dribble moves in every which way. Idan's training was the highest-level version of what my dad had me doing when it came to complex training.

"You're doing pretty good, Chris," Idan would say as I completed drills. "You finished in eight seconds, but Gilbert Arenas did it in six."

"Let's go again!"

I'm super competitive, always, but I wanted to

have my actions do the talking, so I would just grit my teeth and then gun for the six.

As the draft grew near, it had come time for me to start working out for teams—and one of the first teams that came to watch me work out was the Milwaukee Bucks, who had the number one pick in the draft that year. I wasn't sure why the Bucks wanted to see me play, because I knew they already had a great starting point guard in TJ Ford, coming back from a back injury. Idan also let me know that Gilbert was going to come work out with me in front of the Bucks, and I was hyped because I respected him and his game so much. Idan kept telling me how Gil trained, so this would give me a chance to measure myself against him and see how I could get better.

As a seasoned veteran, I now know your body adjusts differently and you train differently in the off-season than during the season. I was just a kid gearing up for the draft, trying to be at peak shape, while Gil could have still been in off-season mode for all I knew.

Idan started us out with some drills to warm up before having me and Gil play one-on-one, from half court, where you only get three dribbles. Not going to lie, I killed Gil all day in front of the Bucks scout. That was a huge deal for my confidence. Back then, young guys didn't get to work out with pros like they do today. The whole time I heard Idan's voice in the back of my head saying, "Gil was one second faster, Gil made two extra shots, Gil got that drill right on the first try!" The Bucks scout looked beyond impressed.

"Great job today," he said, extending for a handshake. I knew they were probably going to go with someone at a different position than me, as they needed size. I was still grateful—they had the first pick and they came to see me. I was glad I impressed them and hoped that would help my stock start to rise.

I was also happy that I got a chance to go hard at one of my favorite players. Even more than that, the fact that Gil took his free time to come help me out, by working out with me, meant the world. He didn't have to wake up early that day, in his off-season, to help me out. He was young, in the NBA, and rich. Gil could have been out on a yacht, spending time with family, or whatever he wanted to be doing, but instead, he spent his free time helping me become better. The respect he showed me was the same kind of respect Papa showed to Happy and George Durham at the shop, the kind of love I was used to getting from my family. This was also one of the first times that I got excited about all of the vets in the NBA who would push me and really have my back. I had no idea about the great teammates and leaders I'd eventually get to learn from over the years, but that little taste gave me all the confidence I needed to keep pushing hard and making sure NBA teams saw what I could do.

A month later, I ended up being selected by the New Orleans Hornets, as the fourth overall pick, in the 2005 NBA draft. I am still to this day extremely thankful to Gil for coming through to help me train and to Idan for training me to put me in the best position possible.

Though I was so happy when I got drafted, I really missed my family when I first got to the NBA. No one ever tells you how lonely the NBA can be at times, especially for a rookie. You are literally by yourself all the time. Coming out of school at such a young age, you also have much older teammates who may have families, children, and hobbies, and many more responsibilities than nineteen- and twenty-year-olds just starting out. Coming from a tight-knit team like Wake Forest, where the team ate every meal together, attended study hall together, practiced together, battled other teams, and shared rooms to getting drafted by the New Orleans Hornets and living in a new city took major adjustments. Thank God for CJ moving in with me when I got drafted. I always had company.

The historic and tragic Hurricane Katrina had devastated New Orleans right before my rookie year. It killed thousands of people and left tens of thousands displaced. As of this writing, it's been seventeen years since it happened, and thousands of people still have never made it back to New Orleans. I remember watching the water overtake homes and completely destroy years and years of businesses and memories. People stood on top of buildings waving for rescue.

As a result of this terrible natural disaster and the damage done to our home arena, we couldn't play in New Orleans my first two seasons. We ended up relocating to Oklahoma City, Oklahoma. I knew a few people in New Orleans that could have made the adjustment a little easier, but I didn't really know anyone in Oklahoma City, where we played our "home" games. Luckily for me, my teammate, JR Smith, the high-flying two guard from New Jersey, became like a real brother to me. He was drafted a year before I was, and lived on the street right next to me, about five hundred yards away.

JR couldn't drive, so I picked him up from his house every day before practice and dropped him off when we finished. I kind of felt like my dad and the way he used to pick up George Durham back in the day. I loved kicking it with JR all day every day and it was rare to see us apart. During those rides, the two of us would talk about the league, our family, our ambitions, and what we wanted to achieve. We became extremely close. As a matter of fact, JR and I got so close, he went on a cruise with my whole family. My family became his family and his family became mine.

Mentorship, yet again, became an ongoing theme for me, especially as a rookie. All of the love

I was given would set the tone for how I treated other players throughout my career. I had true vets like PJ Brown educate me around finances, my diet, professionalism, and what it takes to have a long NBA career. David West was also someone I always paid close attention to.

I remember leaving Coach Prosser's office at Wake Forest one day and walking by Coach Battle's office. I saw David West in there with him. At the time, I was still in college, and D. West was already in the league, playing for the New Orleans Hornets. He had a good relationship with both Coach P and Battle back when he played at Xavier. We were introduced, chopped it up for a minute, and then went about our business. It was great having this moment, because once I got drafted by New Orleans, D West became my teammate, and that made the transition so much easier. There was a built-in mentor waiting for me, and he ended up becoming a close friend and my favorite teammate I've played with my whole career.

D West and I had one of the craziest relationships because we weren't together off the court that much. He didn't play cards or really go out like that. Some guys approach the job like that, they just are quiet and keep to themselves. Despite how differently we approached the social aspect of the league, we just had this crazy chemistry on the court from the mutual respect between us. He and I ended up being on one of the best pick-and-roll duos I think the game has ever seen, and we led in different ways. I am extremely vocal. D West would say something here and there, but he more so used his actions to lead the rest of the team. Our relationship had grown even more after we lost Coach Prosser, and I always valued the kind of leadership he displayed during my early years.

I will also always be grateful to my first head coach in the league, Byron Scott, because he taught me that experience is the best teacher—and gave me the confidence to get on the court and make the mistakes I needed to make in order to learn. That is what community is about, having good people to let you fly, yet keep you grounded and focused.

Focusing sounds easy, but at this level, it can be extremely difficult. Imagine being a twenty-year-old who didn't come from much and didn't have much to lose becoming a famous athlete all of a sudden flooded with millions of dollars. How are kids supposed to know what to do with this new wealth when they've never even met a wealthy person, or have a personal understanding of how to best maximize that kind of salary? There are downsides to this sudden, drastic change. You may end up having a collection of people who don't keep it real with you, or who don't stop you from spending the money in the wrong ways. Community and mentors can help people avoid those pitfalls. We can begin to educate one another, introduce younger kids to financial managers who can help them with the process, and lean on different resources. Outside of my family, my teammates in the NBA challenged me to grow, helped me to remain humble, and directly and indirectly made sure that the money didn't get to my head when I was just starting out.

A few years into my career, and after I had made the NBA All-Star team, I had dinner at a Ruth's Chris Steak House in Woodland Hills, California.

My whole family was there. We enjoyed a really nice meal in celebration of Lil Chris's birthday.

While we were eating, I got a long text from Idan, but this time I was the vet. He was telling me about this amazing guard from Villanova named Josh Hart. When I saw that Idan had started the message with "Remember that time Gil . . . ," I already knew where he was going.

I was now in Gil's position, celebrating my son's birthday in the off-season. I quickly said yes without even hesitating—it was a no-brainer. I was going to be there for Josh, the same way Gil had stepped in for me, the same way Papa stepped up for Happy and countless others.

Idan went on to say that they were meeting about 7:00 or 8:00 a.m. at UCLA's gym in Westwood. I had a full day, so I responded, "Let's make it 6:00 a.m. and I'll be there." I was on Papa time then, waiting in my car at the gym when it was still dark out the next morning.

As vets, we make it happen because we are responsible for showing love to the next generation, the same way the previous generation had pulled up for us. We can always do more, because that's how we build community, that's how we maintain community, and that's how we make sure there will always be that next group of guys to keep our community and legacies going. And hopefully, my showing up to work out that morning will do for Josh what it did for me when Gil was the one showing up. It's moments like these, and the training and other experiences with my AAU kids, that make me grateful for the NBA brotherhood.

19

AN UNTIMELY ENDING

The day after I officially committed to Wake Forest and went to the game with Papa was a Friday. I woke up that morning in the best mood. I'd had an amazing night with him, so the first thing I did was call him and make sure he got home okay the night before. I didn't try him at home. I dialed the number to the station burned in my memory: 723-2232.

"Jones Chevron," Papa answered.

"Papa, it's Chris."

"Hey, Chris, you know, I think you still have my hat from last night. You can keep it."

"Ha, thanks, Papa. I was just calling to say thanks and make sure you made it home safe. You need anything today? I can drop by after school."

"I'm good. You know me, Chris. I'm blessed and highly favored. All good, my man. Didn't you say there was a football game tonight? Go have fun, be with your friends."

"Thanks, Papa."

"Thanks for checking in, but I got a customer pulling up now. Talk to you later. Love you."

"Love you too, Papa."

Papa was right, there *was* a football game that night, and since I had decided not to play football anymore and to focus on basketball, I was excited to see my friends and just hang out in the student section with nothing to worry about.

The day went off like any other day, and then I was finally at the game, which I remember being on a dark, moonless night. I was having a good time under the lights of the field, carefree with my friends. I got a call from CJ around 7:30 p.m., which I thought was weird, because, having just gotten a cell phone, the only people calling me on it at that point were my parents.

"Yo, what up?" I answered.

"I'm on my way back home." It was loud, and I couldn't really hear him, but this confused me.

"Huh? You were just here yesterday. What do you mean you're coming back?"

"Mama said Papa is sick," CJ said.

"Sick? I was just with him last night. He's fine. I even talked to him this morning."

"I don't know. Just telling you what Mama told me."

I was at the end of the big section of bleachers and just immediately knew something was wrong. My chest froze, causing me to take a deep breath and exhale the anxiety. I started walking real fast away from the game and back to my car. On the way, I ran into one of my older cousins, Jeff Jones, who was also at the game. He grabbed me.

"Jeff, what? What happened?" I asked.

"They killed him. They killed your Papa."

I couldn't actually process what he was saying. I just felt my heart drop and I went numb. Killed Papa? I didn't understand. How could that have happened? Who'd killed him? When? I wanted answers and I wanted them immediately. I couldn't understand it and I sure as hell didn't want to believe it.

I was wearing Air Jordan 17s with the little copper plate at the bottom and black snakeskin around the back. There was a fence around the football stadium, behind the bleachers. I kicked that fence so hard that I put a big scuff mark on the toe, breaking the fence.

It was a twenty-five-minute drive to Papa's house. Jeff drove me over there. I was hyperventilating the whole time. I remember rolling the windows down and taking my shirt off to try to get some air and calm down. We got off at the Clemmonsville exit and made a left. Another five to ten seconds later, there was another left, and as soon as I hit his street, I saw nothing but police lights. Imagine the worst movie ever, but you're living it. *Bad dream* doesn't begin to describe it. This was real life. I jumped out of the car and started running down the street. I saw my cousin Sup, and he grabbed me, pulling me into his arms. No one wanted me to look, but I could clearly see a tarp over a body about the size of Papa's in his carport.

My eyes couldn't believe what I was seeing.

Papa's street was just flashing lights, people crying, rain falling, ambulances, sirens, and yellow tape. The whole neighborhood was out there devastated about Papa, trying to piece together what happened, and giving as much information as possible to the cops.

The carport image stuck with me. His body was just lying there facedown with a tarp over it. I'm sure in retrospect my cousin was trying to keep me from seeing that, but I needed to because if I didn't see it then I could never believe he was actually gone. I was breaking down, and I heard Aunt Rhonda, screaming and cussing everybody out. "All you nosy motherfuckers out here, but ain't nobody seen shit!? Y'all see everything else that happens around here, but you didn't see this?! Who the fuck did this?"

Papa's house was still in Belview, and everybody was outside looking. The Belview that my mom grew up in as a little girl was full of working-class parents and manicured green lawns, but recently, it had suffered years of decline, mainly due to people fleeing the area because of all those factory jobs at Reynolds and Hanes relocating to other places. Belview had turned into a rougher neighborhood, just like many places that change over time based on the local industries.

So many things started flashing through my mind in that moment. I thought about sitting next to my granddad at my grandmother's funeral when I was eight—the open casket, Aunt Rhonda losing it, and how Papa gave me a shoulder to cry on. Who would be our shoulder now? Who would keep everyone together? What were we going to do?

I thought about all those days working at the station, listening to Papa tell stories, seeing Papa work on cars with Bo, and the way he cleaned his hands over and over again, attempting to wash away stains that would never disappear. I thought about his tobacco scent and his chattering dentures. I thought about Papa sitting front row at my basketball games, cheering me on, the love he showed when I felt like I did not perform well, the look of pride in his eyes when I was at my highest level, and how he always made CJ and me feel so special.

I thought about his love and how I could tangibly feel it. I thought about his large green-and-white conversion van with the TV inside and how CJ and I used to try to sneak out of church to watch Dallas Cowboys games in it. I thought about how we used to pile up in that van and go on trips everywhere, even as far as Florida—without Papa, of course, because he was working. I thought about Papa letting me drive the Lincoln he also owned and how the door handle had buttons that could unlock the car if you knew the code. I thought about Papa smoking cigarettes, how CJ and I pissed him off when we threw away a pack, trying to protect his lungs. I thought about life. I thought about death and wondered, *Will I be able to make it without Papa?* I heard a scream and was snapped out of my head.

"Who fucking did this!?" Aunt Rhonda continued to yell, the scene double wrapped in yellow crime tape, with more people approaching, "Who fucking did this?!" I didn't know if I'd ever heard Aunt Rhonda curse before, but that situation certainly called for it.

Papa lived on a busy street. Somebody had to have seen something. Everybody knew our family in Winston-Salem. A lot of people thought my family were like the Huxtables, from *The Cosby Show,* a middle-class Black family who would stay away from drama, but let's be clear, we had cousins and uncles all around the city who were more than ready to figure everything out without the police.

"Y'all better find them dudes before we do," my cousin Reggie said to my uncle Jerome, my dad's brother who was also a police officer. "I'm telling you, man."

Uncle Jerome tried to calm him down to no avail.

CJ was driving back, but he hadn't been told any of the details. He found out with about an hour left to go in his trip.

I heard people telling cops, "Yo, y'all better find out who did this," over and over again.

Finally, there was nothing more for us to do, standing on Moravia Street in front of Papa's house. All of us with faces wet from tears.

We all left and did what we do: we met up at a church close to Papa's house. I finally saw my mom, who had been working a late shift, CJ, my dad, and we all just embraced and held each other, praying that this nightmare wasn't real. But it was.

In the days to come, we started piecing together what had happened, but that didn't make it any easier.

After a long day and a week of excitement, with me committing to Wake, Papa pulled up in his driveway and began unloading groceries that he'd picked up. As he was taking a bag out of the trunk, five teenage boys allegedly surrounded him. Did they target him beforehand because of the station or was it the wad of cash in his pocket? Otherwise, why would they do it? Papa took care of everybody. There were so many people who came to the service station. They didn't have enough money to get their car fixed or couldn't pay it down, but they needed their vehicle for work. Papa never judged them or offered unfair loans. He would just suck it up and fix their cars and tried to get them on a payment plan. I can't imagine how much debt he never collected on. He was that kind of person.

That alone made him a legend and so valuable to the community, protected even. Or, rather, he should have been.

I keep going back to these guys who did this to Papa and what was going through their minds. They clearly didn't know who this man was that they went after. They could have just strong-armed him by going into his pockets, stealing his cash, and continuing with their night, but they did so much more. They killed him. The kids, maybe from my area and maybe not, tied his hands behind his back and duct-taped his mouth shut before viciously beating him in his head and on his face with metal pipes. As if he were the bad guy, as if he were the one blocking their hopes and dreams, as if he would ever do anything to harm them, as if he weren't an elderly deacon who worked hard at taking care of his family and community.

It's hard not to blame the change we had seen in the area he was living in, how it had become so different, but that's too easy.

There were times growing up, after my grandma died and Papa was living by himself all the way across town, when we tried to get him to move in with us, but he wasn't having it. He wanted his own space, I get it. At the time, I didn't understand it, but now I see that he couldn't leave the neighborhood that made him. He believed strongly that staying there, helping the people around him, and making a difference was his obligation. I still can't believe he lost his life in that same damn neighborhood.

Papa, my grandfather, whom I will forever be proud of, had heart trouble. The combination of the beating, the uncertainty, and the fear caused cardiac arrhythmia, which led to his untimely demise. All for his wallet. Money he just would have given them. All they had to do was ask. Everyone else did.

Papa was only sixty one when he passed. Sixty-one.

Papa was the rock of our entire family. He was the rock of the community. He was my best friend in the world.

Everybody in the world seemed like they were at our house the next few days. The service station was closed. I don't remember when it reopened. And I still don't remember some things that took place between Papa's death and the actual funeral. I feel like I just cried so much, I wasn't processing everything in real time. It would have been different if he wasn't so young. It would have been different if he'd died of natural causes or died of lung cancer like so many of the people in Winston-Salem that we knew. We would have had time to begin to process things, but to have his life end that particular way, shortened the way it was just days after the best night the two of us had shared together, crushed me. Sixty-one years of age. He had so much more life to enjoy. We should have had so many more years to enjoy him. Sixty-one and thriving—it shouldn't have been the end.

The days following something that traumatic, after the adrenaline wears off, are days when you just sleep. I finally woke up, hoping it hadn't happened. It happened Friday night, so Saturday and Sunday, we were out of school. Monday was the eighteenth, and the funeral was Tuesday the nineteenth. I don't even know if I went to school. People always say "I know how you feel" to people going through a hard time. In my experience, no, they don't. Everyone's situations around loss are different and I learned from Papa how to handle these times. When George or Bo or any of the Jones Disciples would be dealing with their issues and having a hard time, remembering tragedies or traumas in their past, Papa would say one thing, not "I know how you feel," but "I'm here to listen if you want to talk about it." In the wake of Papa's passing, that might have been the lesson I was thinking about the most.

A lot of preparations were made for the funeral. We knew it'd be big, so we had to make sure everything was in place. In fact, Dreamland wasn't even big enough to fit everyone. We had to move it over to Cleveland Avenue, to the biggest church in the whole city. It felt like everybody showed up to show their love. The entire Wake Forest basketball team even came. I didn't even go to school there yet, but Coach Prosser and the whole team came out to show their support. Funerals are so hard for me so this support meant so much. Funerals always conjured up memories of when Grandma Rachel passed and how difficult that was. I had sat next to Papa, who told me to be strong for my mother, and now there we were, burying him.

The whole funeral felt dark—too dark for me to want to be part of, but this was for Papa. Even all these years later, I have a lot of trouble with death. There's always a coldness that blankets the room—full of sad, wet faces in every direction. People appear to be visibly broken beyond repair. Boxes and packs of tissue circulate. You see obituaries, which are normally on printed programs highlighting a picture of the departed, with a short bio, schedule, a poem written by someone's niece, and a list of the remaining family members. The worst part of funerals that always freaked me out the most were the open caskets. Imagine being a child and looking at a lifeless body that you once spent so much time with, knowing that person will never again hug you, say "I love you," ever again.

These bodies normally make their debut at funeral homes, where everybody says the same thing: "Oh, the mortician did such a great job—that body looks so nice," which is a lie, because those bodies never look nice; the idea of this is creepy. And then they make their way to the church, where everybody gets one last look before the casket is closed—most of the time causing multiple family members to experience the biggest breakdowns.

When they closed the casket at my grandma's funeral, Aunt Rhonda lost it. There was no way to contain her as her hurt and pain spilled out of her eyes and over her hands, and then onto the clothes of people hugging her, trying to help her deal with the pain. There's something about the open casket shutting that sets people off and intensifies the hurt. But we were at Papa's, and the casket was wide open. He was wearing one of his church suits, but that's honestly all I remember about how he looked. I didn't want that image of him burned into my brain. I wanted to choose to remember him as the guy who took me to the Wake game a few nights before, the only guy strong enough to start his own service station when nobody thought he could.

However, there is one image burned in my brain from the scene at Papa's funeral. At one point, everybody was just sitting there in the pews: my mom, dad, uncles, aunts, cousins, everyone in the church was sitting down, mourning, listening to the choir sing "My Soul Has Been Anchored." My mom just stood up, kind of hunched over and shaky. You could tell everything she had was taken out of her. Her soul was crushed. I wanted to hug her, to show that I felt her pain as well—that was usually Papa's job, but not anymore. I was stuck, we all were stuck as she stood alone, with the weight of the world on her shoulders, in pain, but leaning on her faith enough to push forward. She stretched her arms out, looking up as if she just wanted to hug her mom and dad one last time.

Our family along with so many community members made our way back to Papa's after the funeral. This was a tradition after funerals for us. There was enough chicken to feed the whole state of North Carolina twice, fried, baked, and whatever else you can think of, on top of turkey legs, collard greens, sweet potatoes, macaroni and cheese, and all kinds of cakes and pies. There was so much chicken that we overdosed and I couldn't eat it for weeks.

AN UNTIMELY ENDING

Everyone was sending food, trying to help, but then, life has to keep moving on. It's sad, but it's true. People die, even tragically, and you still have to get up and do your work, keep things moving, and be there for the people around you. That's what we did.

One of the hardest things for me to focus on was wondering how my mother was going to cope. She was Papa's oldest daughter, close to his heart, and she loved him dearly, eagerly ready to show him affection every chance she got.

I couldn't stop thinking about the sound of her voice waking me up every morning as she laughed and traded stories with Papa and Aunt Rhonda—about the church and how that no-good lady was trying to get close to Papa, and about the service station, about CJ and me growing up so fast, and about her job and about so many other things. If Mom and Papa didn't have work, those conversations would have gone on for hours. Their morning talks were filled with an abundance of joy and overhearing them was always a pleasant way to start my day.

The idea that I wouldn't hear my mother's laugh on one of those conference calls in the morning again or the sound of her voice or the excitement that filled up inside her when she spoke to Papa terrified me, but I knew I had to be strong for us all. Papa would have done the same thing.

While thinking about my mother and how she was going to deal, I fell into a space, remembering that I was going to need a way to heal as well. I thought sports and other activities could take my mind off what had happened. I did try to stay busy, and I would like to think it worked for a time, but eventually, we all have to face those feelings.

I think the hardest part for me to wrap my head around was that everyone in the community knew Papa, and no one in their right mind would ever try to harm him. None of that mattered, though—not Papa's community service, not his role at Dreamland, not anything—because it still happened.

There are many ways to deal with grief, like talking about it, or therapy—we did neither, which probably wasn't the smartest thing. Outside of staying busy, another way of dealing that has worked for me was collecting things that reminded me of Papa. Before the funeral, I went over to his house and looked through some of his things. I had already had a few things that belonged to him, things I've managed to hold on to over the years—but nothing screamed Papa like his gold watch. I saw it sitting on the counter and instantly put it on.

I believe it was called Twist-O-Flex. And it really wasn't gold, more like gold plated with the elastic kind of stretchy band that would leave an imprint on your wrist after you took it off. Papa wore it all the time, and I decided I'd carry it with me from then on. I wore that watch every day for a long time, just so I could have a piece of him with me. That watch, along with the Wake Forest cap that Papa gave me on the day I signed, were my prized possessions—artifacts, evidence that he was once here with me.

20

GAME OVER

- - - - - - - - - - - - - - - - - - - -

Parkland High School, Winston-Salem
Parkland vs. West Forsyth High
November 20, 2002

"CP, you got fifty-nine!" one of my teammates yelled.
I knew I was hot, but I didn't know I was that hot.
And this wasn't fifty-nine from a hundred shots because everybody was feeding me or from gunnin'
every time I touched it. I had a triple-double going

as well and was filling up the whole stat sheet. We got back out there after the short time-out, we ran a play on the inbound, and I got the ball again. I started dribbling, and took the ball down the court.

My mind was as clear as day. I had fifty-nine points.

As I pushed the ball up the left side of the court, I began to weave in and out of the defense as I made my way to the right side of the lane. I hesitated to see the court like I had my whole life, and I saw an opening. I drove the lane, split the defenders, felt the center closing in, and put up a floater before their center's body collided into mine. The bucket dropped, and then I fell. I lay there for a second, realizing that I had just achieved something that I would never top.

Sixty-one. Sixty-one points. The whistle blew. I got fouled by that center, and had an and-1 opportunity.

I was six points away from MJ's state record of sixty-seven with ninety seconds to go. That number was in reach and would mean my name passed the greatest to ever do it and would be in the state's record books for who knew how long.

This was all going through my mind as I walked to the free throw line. I closed my eyes and took a breath to center myself. The ref bounced me the ball. So many of my family members and friends, especially people who were connected to Papa, filled the stands. Emotions flooded my body. All my thoughts were about Papa: the lessons he taught me, the time I spent at the gas station, when he found out I was going to Wake Forest, the way he passed me the hat, when I learned about what happened to him, the trauma, the pain, the confusion, my family, and how I would never see him again.

I took a deep breath. The deepest breath I'd ever taken.

I took one dribble. Papa was my best friend, is my best friend, and forever will be.

Without getting into my free throw shooting motion, I picked up the ball and threw it directly out of bounds.

I walked off the court. I saw my dad and immediately collapsed into his arms crying. Crying from exhaustion. Crying from relief. Crying for Papa.

Sixty-one. RIP, Papa Chilly. Love you for life.

21

REST IN POWER, PAPA

- -

YOU WILL FACE MANY DEFEATS IN LIFE, BUT
NEVER LET YOURSELF BE DEFEATED.

—MAYA ANGELOU

During every game I played at Wake Forest, I
held a laminated copy of Papa's obituary in my
hand while the national anthem was performed.
It read . . .

Philippians 4:13: "I can do all things through Christ who strengthens me."

Mr. Nathaniel "Chilly" Frederick Jones departed this life Friday, Nov. 15, 2002, unexpectedly at his residence at 905 Moravia Street. He was born March 22, 1941, in Winston-Salem to the late Willie and Roma Jones. He was a graduate of Carver High School, Class of 1959. His lifetime is reflected in self-employment at Jones Chevron for 38 years (the only black private owned service station in the state of North Carolina) and Christian membership at Dreamland Park his entire life, serving as past chairman and member of the deacon board, program director of the usher board and member of the male chorus and Sunday school. He was preceded in death by his wife, Rachel H. Jones, in February 1993.

Family love and devotion is instilled in the memory of him by two loving daughters, Robin J. Paul (Charles) and Rhonda J. Richardson (Antonio); four devoted grandsons, Charles Paul Jr., Christopher Paul, Reginald Richardson and Antonio Richardson Jr., and a devoted granddaughter, Tequoia Richardson; three sisters, Elveta Rutledge of Washington, D.C., Esther Haggler (Joseph) of Oakton, Va., and Hattie Jones of Capitol Heights, Md.; seven brothers, James Jones, Hubert Jones, Odell Jones (Rosalyn) and Hobart Jones (Carolyn), all of Winston-Salem, Thomas Jones (Rosa) of Ayers, Mass., George Jones (Patricia) of Raleigh and Reginald Jones (Ethel) of Walkertown; a brother-in-law, Roscoe J. Hines (Joann) of Mount Airy; devoted friends, Hazel Gilbert, Aldrena Gaither, Mr. and Mrs. Hunter Hill, Willie "Bo" Crawford; a godson, Deron Simmons; and a host of nieces, nephews, other relatives and many other devoted friends. Anytime you met him and asked, "How are you?" his response was, "I am blessed and highly favored in the Lord."

Funeral services will be held on Tuesday, Nov. 19, 2002, at 1:30 p.m. from the Greater Cleveland Avenue Christian Church, with the Rev. Ronald Fisher officiating.

SIXTY-ONE

Burial will be in the family plot of the Piedmont Memorial Park. The family visitation will be from noon to 1:30 p.m. Tuesday at the church. In lieu of flowers, donations can be made to Dreamland Park Baptist Church Building Fund.

—Published by *Winston-Salem Journal*

from November 18–19, 2002

You know a lot of the rest. I was drafted to the NBA. I have been so blessed to have had a successful NBA career. There's a Chevron logo on every Jordan Brand pair of shoes I've designed so that when I play, I'm honoring Papa. My family, especially Papa, made me who I am today. Every day, I try to live through his values and make him proud.

22

THE AFTERMATH

THE TOP OF ONE MOUNTAIN IS THE BOTTOM
OF THE NEXT, SO KEEP CLIMBING.
—MARIANNE WILLIAMSON

Oklahoma City, Oklahoma, 2020. It'd been almost twenty years since Papa passed. Reporters had started asking about his murder now that one of the key witnesses recanted her testimony. It hit me in a certain way and brought back a lot of bad memories of that time period. I felt so bad for my family, especially my mom and Aunt Rhonda, who had to relive that horrible experience.

As reporters started to ask questions, the pain I felt, the pain CJ felt, holding my mom and Aunt Rhonda, all came back to me—and then fast-forward to my reality, where talking heads and reporters think it's completely okay to play around with other people's trauma and the darkest things from their past, just so they can have a headline. But I know my values and how Papa raised me, so I always try to be the bigger person. I also thought back to George Durham, the young man from the neighborhood whom Papa took in after he got out of jail. Second chances are a real thing.

The Innocence Project had reopened my grandfather's case. What's even more interesting is that Papa's murder was the second case that the Innocence Project in North Carolina took an interest in, the first being the murder of James Jordan Sr., Michael Jordan's father. I'm not saying that they are focusing on us because of who we are; it is just extremely odd until you consider the work that these organizations do and how they are historically underfunded.

The Innocence Project filed to a special commission, with the intention of opening the case back up, which was tough for my family. The hearings were set to begin right before COVID shocked the world, locking everything down and sending us into quarantine. The alleged killers still got their day in court, and I watched the entire hearing online, learning so many things that I didn't know back when I was seventeen. The most painful part about it was seeing my mom and Aunt Rhonda have to relive all of that trauma as the old wounds were opened, one by one. As a family, we had to cover my mom and aunt with love, in an effort to protect them from the past—the kind of things that reporters don't see.

I saw four of the five boys that were convicted in individual trials in 2004 and 2005 for the first time in seventeen years. They were all so young like I was at the time, but now grown men, aged in a way that only the system can do.

SIXTY-ONE

I never studied psychology, and I don't know what the five stages of grief are and all of that, but the one feeling that I could identify with was anger. Papa's death left me with enough anger and rage for a lifetime. Sometimes that anger will come out on the court or in disagreements with my friends or the kind of frustration that arises when you're trying to complete a difficult task. Realizing that the anger would never bring Papa back was the only way I was able to move forward and start that healing process. I am continuing to understand this in a deeper way through therapy.

I often think about jail and prison. I've read books, heard speeches, viewed studies, and watched every single television show you can think of that deals with the idea of jail. Obviously, I think jail is for some really damaged and cruel people, but I keep going back to how old those kids were, fourteen and fifteen. Kids. My heart will never believe that sending someone that age away for fifty years is a good idea. It took me a long time to get there.

I understand that people make bad decisions, terrible decisions that can seem impossible to come back from—but if you learn from it and are trying to make amends with the people you hurt, then you should get a second chance. That is redemption, and our society lacks that. We send people to jail, almost guarantee they don't get the resources that they need to be productive, and then they come home, still feeling like they don't have a stake in society—which basically gives them the license, and almost dares them, to be reckless. Then we sit back and blame them for society's failures.

I thought about them, their reality and what they've been through.

Troubling information began to surface as Papa's alleged killers' hearing began. For starters, Jessicah Black, who was the key witness at the time, recanted her entire testimony at the hearing. Her statement was needed to convict the boys, who were now men, and now she was just taking it back.

Black had originally testified at trial, saying that she drove the five young men around that night, through the park and near Moravia Street, where Papa lived. Black said she heard them going on and on about finding someone to rob, and then even said she heard them beat Papa to death. Black is now saying all of that was made up, that the police forced her to say that, just as they forced the boys to confess, and she followed suit because they threatened her with jail time if she didn't.

Beyond that young woman's testimony, the main thing that caught the young men in Papa's killing is that one of them used his credit card. No one brought that up during the hearing, which frustrated me greatly.

The original trial started during my sophomore year of college, which was about two years after the incident. I really wanted to attend the trial and be there to support my mom and Aunt Rhonda, the way Papa would have wanted me to. But both of my parents said no, because there was already too much drama surrounding the case. The lawyers for the boys began to call them "the Winston-Salem 5" because they were so young, and there were five of them just like in the infamous Central Park case, many years prior. They were trying to get the case moved because they felt like my public stature would deny them a fair trial. My presence would have complicated things, and all the parties involved wanted to avoid that.

In addition, the lawyers representing Papa's alleged killers have now introduced new suspects, which means the person or people who may have actually done it have been free all this time and were never held accountable.

One thing I do know: Papa, my best friend and biggest influence, deserves justice—not manufactured justice, but the real kind of justice needed to truly give our family some sense of peace. I thought we had that seventeen years ago, but, again, it had painfully resurfaced.

My family finally now has closure and justice for Papa.

On April 28th, 2022, the three-judge panel ruled that the defense did not prove the claimants' innocence. The verdict was upheld. My mom and Aunt Rhonda were so brave speaking at the proceedings. We finally feel closure and that justice was served.

23

A DIFFERENCE

- - - - - - - - - - - - - - - - - -

THE SMALLEST ACT OF KINDNESS IS WORTH
MORE THAN THE GRANDEST INTENTION.
—OSCAR WILDE

One of the things that allowed me to go on was learning to focus on my grandfather's legacy instead of being crippled by the tragedy. Papa taught me the importance of hard work, taking care of your family, building community, and, most importantly, the value of being strategic. Because you can't take care of your family, or work hard at anything, if you don't have a plan.

I always knew the lessons that Papa dropped on me were important, and that's evident considering my journey. Papa's humble nature and work ethic have guided me through my career. As president of the National Basketball Players Association, I thought a lot about his lessons. Through it all, his confidence in me gave me confidence in myself.

None of these accomplishments was a mistake or the result of some pipe dream. They are all results of strategic planning. The kind of planning that will continue to pay dividends throughout the rest of my basketball career, after I retire and hopefully spill over to my next chapter in business. I feel blessed to be able to use the fruits of my labor in an effort to uplift and empower people who look like I do.

Like I do every day, I was guided by Papa's values on May 25, 2020, the day after Lil Chris's birthday, when a Black man named George Floyd, also known as "Big Boy Floyd," made his way into Cup Foods, a grocery store at the intersection of East Thirty-Eighth Street and Chicago Avenue in the Powderhorn Park neighborhood of Minneapolis, to purchase a pack of cigarettes.

Floyd was having a rough day and got into an altercation with a store employee, who walked up on his car minutes after he made the transaction to accuse him of using a counterfeit twenty-dollar bill. A minor altercation ensued. The police were called, and soon after they arrived, Floyd was hemmed up on the ground in cuffs. You know what happened next. George Floyd's murder would alter history and leave our country, rich in systemic racism, permanently transformed.

From Philando Castile, Walter Scott, and Freddie Gray to Laquan McDonald and Michael Brown—America has disgustingly become used to seeing the last minutes of Black men's lives, or their actual deaths, on camera. These killings happen, and then the videos are circulated online to be shared and reshared and talked about and commented on billions of times. But Floyd's murder was different. For one, Floyd had a digital footprint so people could learn about him—because he put out music as a rapper with the Screwed Up Click and had played college basketball. That meant anyone who googled his name could actually see him happy and alive and free—in a way that humanized his journey and instantly delivered empathy to anyone in search of who he really was. On top of that, the deadly coronavirus pandemic had shut down the world, killing millions of people. It instantly pushed us into the most challenging time we've ever seen in our lives. COVID-19 paralyzed us, closing schools, businesses, sporting events, and the world as we knew it.

Everybody was home, getting serious cases of cabin fever, with their eyes locked on their TV screens for large portions of the day—and if they weren't watching whatever news channel they subscribe to, then they were tapped into social media—anxious to see how we would combat this deadly virus. The video of Floyd hit the internet—lying on the ground in cuffs, gasping for air, while veteran police officer Derek Chauvin kneeled on his neck. He treated Floyd as if he wasn't a person, for more than nine minutes—and the world saw it. Those in the Black community were rightfully upset because we have been aware of this kind of policing for years; however, this was one of the first times people outside of our communities got a chance to see what we go through and what we fear. They couldn't change the channel, because it was on every station and plastered across all their social media accounts. The entire country was forced to watch this man die on camera, while calling for his mother, all over a pack of cigarettes and an alleged fake twenty-dollar bill.

Weeks and weeks of protest and riots followed as citizens representing every nationality, ethnicity, and gender took to the streets. It was like the world finally woke up, after hundreds of years, and realized how hard it is to be Black in America.

As NBA players, in a league that is predominantly Black, many eyes were fixed on us, wondering what we were going to do to address the disparities that African Americans face. Even though we aren't politicians, we know we have a platform to use our voice, and our talents have propelled us to be resources and leaders in our communities.

While change was in the air, the NBA decided to play a role in helping to educate coaches, players, and other staff. We were settling into Florida inside what became known as the *NBA bubble*. The bubble brought our teams to the ESPN Wide World of Sports Complex in Orlando, Florida. We were locked down in quarantine so that we could finish the 2019–2020 season. No one came in, and no one could go out. We just played our games and basically went back to our hotel rooms, night after night. It was lonely and it was hard and it was challenging.

The NBA and NBPA executives, in response to Floyd's murder and what we were going through, had tried to shine a light on the issues we all faced as they relate to systemic racism and how we as a league could effect change. They placed copies of Michelle Alexander's brilliant book on the prison-industrial complex, *The New Jim Crow*, in everybody's room inside of the bubble. Too many people believe that jail is just a place for unredeemable humans, but Alexander explains how easy it is for an innocent Black person to end up in the system and never get out. The book is a beautiful collection of stories.

"Arguably the most important parallel between mass incarceration and Jim Crow is that both have served to define the meaning and significance of race in America," Alexander wrote. "Indeed, a primary function of any racial caste system is to define the meaning of race in its time. Slavery defined what it meant to be black (a slave), and Jim Crow defined what it meant to be black (a second-class citizen). Today mass incarceration defines the meaning of blackness in America: black people, especially black men, are criminals. That is what it means to be black."

I am always inspired that I can be part of a brotherhood with voices that are powerful and that takes responsibility for social justice, especially as a person who cares deeply about these issues. It feels good to know that our players understand the power of unity. The books would be a great start, but as president of the NBPA and knowing how strongly the players felt about the situation, we knew that we had to do much more.

What would Papa do?

We came to a solution that we felt would make a powerful statement. *Everyone pays attention to the NBA and the messages we put out, so instead of our names going on the backs of our jerseys, maybe every player should be able to share an important message.*

Imagine the best basketball players in the world, with a stage like no other, able to remind you throughout an entire game, over and over and over, about a message that was important to them. The world would be forced to see our diverse collection of messages and ideas; after all, everyone was in the house watching the games—even non-fans tuned in because in a pandemic, no one was leaving home.

This wasn't something that had ever happened in the league before, but this was also not something that happened around the country before. This wasn't going to be easy to actually make happen. We soon realized there were a lot of challenges in leaving the messages open ended. What if a guy wanted to put FU*K TRUMP on his back, they'd have to block that. Losing the message over divisive language was not our goal.

After all, this was about social justice, the same kind of social justice that paused the league after Jacob Blake's shooting. And if these issues were strong enough to stop us from playing the game we love and have dedicated our lives to, then they will hold weight on the back of our jerseys. With that in mind, we were able to come up with a few social justice messages such as:

- BLACK LIVES MATTER
- ANTI RACIST
- LISTEN TO US
- EDUCATION REFORM
- I AM A MAN
- SAY HER NAME
- I CAN'T BREATHE
- JUSTICE NOW
- ALLY
- EQUALITY

I was so conflicted about my own messaging that I switched three times. At first, I went with PEACE, before switching to SAY HER NAME. Then I thought about it and settled on EQUALITY. If EQUALITY is on the back of my jersey, then I would be able to speak on any and everything. We have a serious problem with policing and racism in this country, but there are other issues too, like housing, education, and dealing with food deserts, and I wanted to address them all. If my main message was EQUALITY, there would be no way to box the message in.

This moment gave me a chance to reflect on all of the things I've been a part of in the NBA, and one of the most impactful was the banning of Clippers owner Donald Sterling back in 2013. We talked about possibly boycotting a playoff game and how to make a statement against what we knew was wrong. I drew on that experience when working through the complexities of the bubble and when working with my fellow players to decide whether or not to continue to play after Jacob Blake was shot.

It's crazy to think that just four years before that, I stood with LeBron James, Dwyane Wade, and

Carmelo Anthony during the 2016 ESPYs to take a stand in the sports world about the Black Lives Matter movement and why it's crucial for our fans to support it. Our foundation is always working toward leveling the playing field for communities in need. My personal team is always working to support, uplift, and empower HBCUs. Instead of just finishing my degree at Wake, I wanted to be a part of the HBCU community myself as a student at Winston-Salem State University, and graduated with my degree in communications. I'm so proud to rep an HBCU in that way and I even carry my school ID around in my wallet. It's important not just to talk about the work, but to roll your sleeves up and do it.

Strategy. This is what we learned from Papa. We worked together as players and governors on what we wanted to get done. We were strategic in creating the social justice coalition and put $300 million toward social justice initiatives.

At the end of the day, this is a story about a man who meant a lot to me who was a Black business owner. We also need to focus on supporting Black businesses day in and day out.

As the NBA rolled out its plans, a few of the

Black leaders from the MLS (Major League Soccer) reached out and wanted to do a call. We had a great conversation with them, which was refreshing because most leagues tend to stay in their own lanes. We spoke for an hour or so, and they were fighting the same battles we were, especially in the areas of hiring. At the time, the MLS only had two Black coaches and two Black GMs in the entire league.

We connected on the idea of performing visual acts that promoted unity, and that energized me tremendously. We were speaking the same language. Justin Morrow mentioned one of their guys wanted to design a shirt. We loved that idea ourselves, because we have so many diverse players with more talents than just putting a ball in the basket. I called Russell Westbrook to see if he and his fashion brand, Honor the Gift, wanted to be a part of it.

Everything we were working on was giving meaning to the bubble. We felt like we were helping empower the Black community during such a tough moment. Many of our fans are kids, so they don't know about the money being spent, the businesses we are helping, and how that will lead to

Black opportunities for years to come. As a matter of fact, many of our adult fans aren't paying attention to things like that—they just want to see a good game. What they did see, while watching that game, is players like us promoting unity, equality, and a host of other social justice issues. They will know that we care, and hopefully it will lead them to care too. And that is what *Sixty-One* is about: caring and advocating.

These lessons I learned from Papa equipped me to deal with complex conversations with friends, while engaging the MLS, making sure I'm doing my job helping players as best as I can. This all while handling my responsibility as a professional athlete, and balancing family life with Jada and the kids at home. I am able to do this because I had Nathaniel "Papa Chilly" Jones as a mentor, a boss, and as a powerful influence who just happened to be my grandfather, my papa.

EPILOGUE: PAPA'S LEGACY

WHEN A MAN HAS DONE WHAT HE CONSIDERS
TO BE HIS DUTY TO HIS PEOPLE AND HIS COUNTRY,
HE CAN REST IN PEACE. I BELIEVE I HAVE MADE
THAT EFFORT AND THAT IS, THEREFORE,
WHY I WILL SLEEP FOR THE ETERNITY.
—NELSON MANDELA

I never really think about it like this, but at thirty-eight years old, I have now been on this earth for more years without Papa than the seventeen we spent together. And he manages still to be my biggest influence. Every time I'm in a tough situation or forced to make a decision, *What would Papa do?* dances across my mind, and then quickly the correct answer comes.

I can look back now and smile, thinking about all the things Papa has done for me. And even though the thought of his death still hurts, I am able to continuously push forward because of the memory of the time I spent with him.

On bad days, I stress out about the fact that he never saw me put on a college or NBA jersey. And I know he looked down and smiled when I won Rookie of the Year, or led the league in assists, or led the league in steals, or brought home a couple of gold medals. I wonder if he'd have words for me when I lose my cool or get into it with refs. I can't imagine how loud he was cheering when I made it to the NBA Finals.

As my career has progressed, and doors have opened up for me to use my platform to tell stories, I always end up thinking about Papa and what he taught me. Beyond my NBA career, I've begun to be excited about being a storyteller. The first place I decided to draw from is my experiences, so I've been thinking and looking back at Papa, our story, and what he taught me about work ethic, family, faith, fatherhood, leadership, community, and making your own way. There are so many universal truths he taught me, and I want to use this book to share them with family, friends, and fans for the first time.

I know this book was probably difficult to read in some ways, as it is filled with a lot of heartache, but I crafted it with love. As hard as some of this is to retell, these experiences helped make me who I am. I hope that my story will move and inspire people to be their best for the people around them. I've always said that I've become the person I am because of the people around me, and this book clearly illustrates that.

My grandpa had to delegate all kinds of things in dealing with his family, his friends, and work, and he handled it with ease while taking time to pass those lessons down to me. And now, I'm so proud that I get a chance to share these lessons with you.

Papa's legacy deserves to live on forever, and I have been trying to make that one of my main priorities since I came into the NBA.

In 2005, I launched a philanthropic campaign designed to highlight Papa's spirit and the Winston-Salem community. I established the Nathaniel Jones Student Scholarship at Wake Forest, which assists students with financial need, with preference first to graduates of West Forsyth or Winston Salem Forsyth County Schools System second to a basketball player at Wake Forest. My family and I also created the CP3 Partnership in conjunction with the Winston-Salem Foundation to support charitable causes such as Habitat for Humanity, the Make-A-Wish Foundation, Feed the Children, and many more.

Papa was special!! I wrote this book to give you a little insight into a relationship that was built on trust, love, and the belief that superheroes really do exist. I hope this book encourages you to continue to be one or to find your own.

ACKNOWLEDGMENTS

- -

Thank you to anyone and everyone who has helped me along my journey from the young boy you just read about up to the man I am today. There are too many names to name and I don't want to miss anyone so I'll just say, you all know who you are. Thank you for the support, encouragement, and love along the way. Peace.